PIANO · VOCAL · GUITAR

LEAN ON ME
Songs of Unity, Courage & Hope

ISBN 978-1-70510-542-9

Visit Hal Leonard Online at
www.halleonard.com

Contact Us:
Hal Leonard
7777 West Bluemound Road
Milwaukee, WI 53213
Email: info@halleonard.com

In Europe, contact:
Hal Leonard Europe Limited
42 Wigmore Street
Marylebone, London, W1U 2RN
Email: info@halleonardeurope.com

In Australia, contact:
Hal Leonard Australia Pty. Ltd.
4 Lentara Court
Cheltenham, Victoria, 3192 Australia
Email: info@halleonard.com.au

AT THE SAME TIME

Words and Music by
ANN HAMPTON CALLAWAY

Moderate Ballad

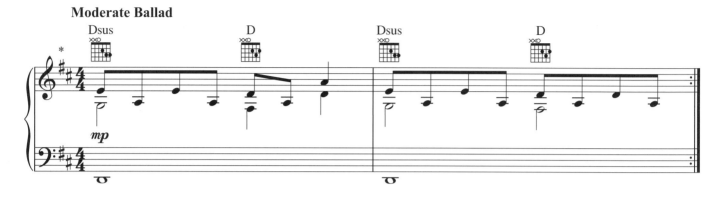

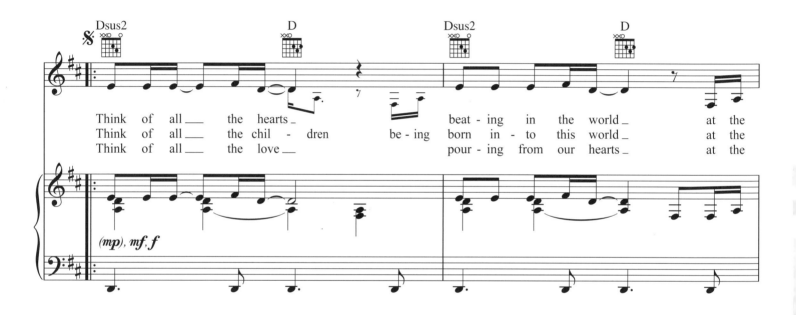

Think of all ___ the hearts ___ beat-ing in the world ___ at the
Think of all ___ the chil-dren be-ing born in-to this world ___ at the
Think of all ___ the love ___ pour-ing from our hearts ___ at the

same time. ___
same time. ___
same time. ___

* *Recorded a half step lower.*

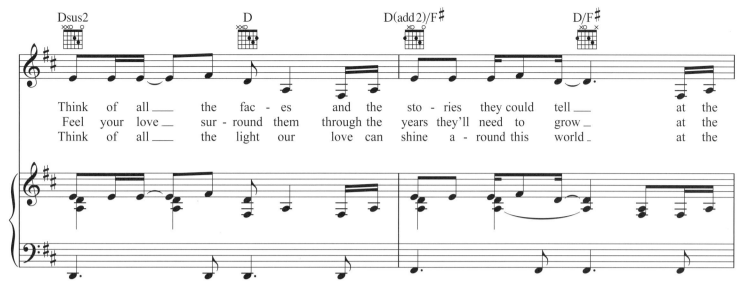

Think of all ____ the fac - es and the sto - ries they could tell ____ at the
Feel your love ____ sur - round them through the years they'll need to grow ____ at the
Think of all ____ the light our love can shine a - round this world ____ at the

same time. ____
same time. ____
same time. ____

Think of all ____ the eyes ____ look - ing out ____ in - to ____ this world, ____
Think of all ____ the hands ____ that will be reach - ing for ____ a dream. ____
Think what we've been giv - en ____ and then think what we ____ could lose. ____

trying to make __ some sense of what we see.

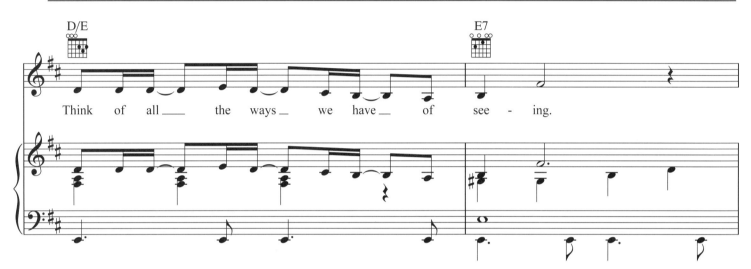

Think of all ___ the ways __ we have __ of see - ing.

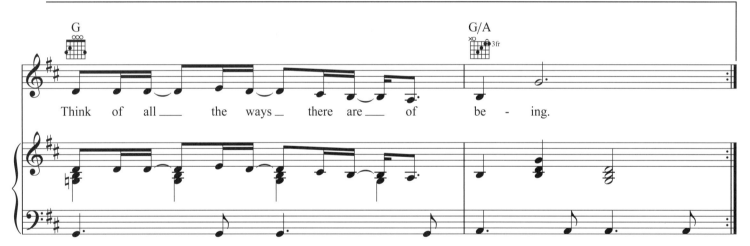

Think of all ___ the ways __ there are ___ of be - ing.

Think of all ___ the dreams that could come true ___

All of life ___ is in our trem - bling hands. ___ It's time to

bor - row. _____ The time has come _ to be _ a fam - i - ly. _

D.S. al Coda

Oh. _____

CODA

build a world _ that loves and un - der - stands. _____

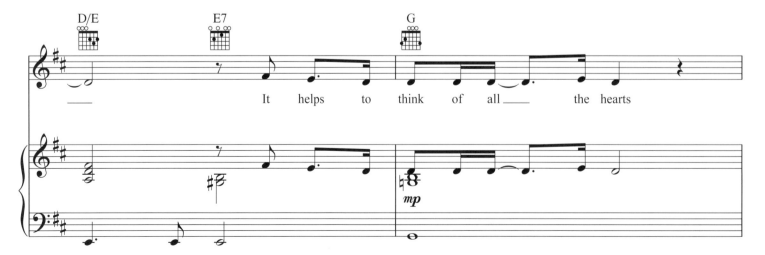

It helps to think of all __ the hearts

BE A LIGHT

Words and Music by THOMAS RHETT,
JOSH MILLER, JOSH THOMPSON
and MATTHEW DRAGSTREM

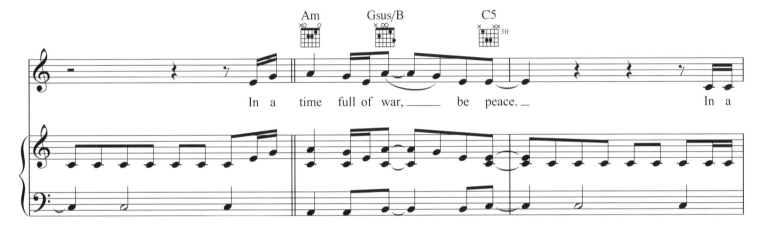

In a time full of war, ____ be peace. ____ In a

time full of doubt, ___ just be - lieve. ____ Yeah, there ain't _

____ that much dif - f'rence be - tween ____ you and me. In a

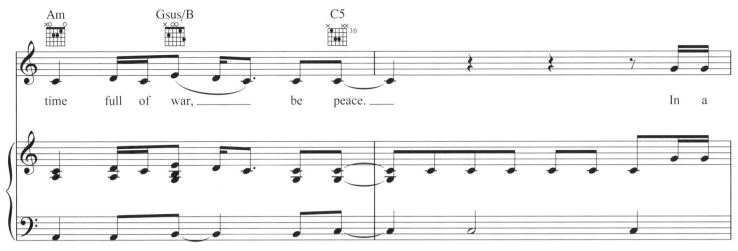

time full of war, _____ be peace. _____ In a

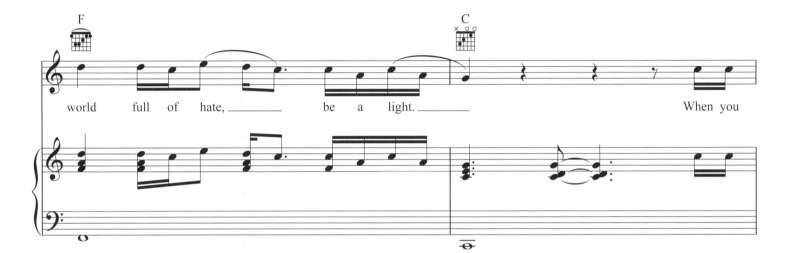

world full of hate, _____ be a light. _____ When you

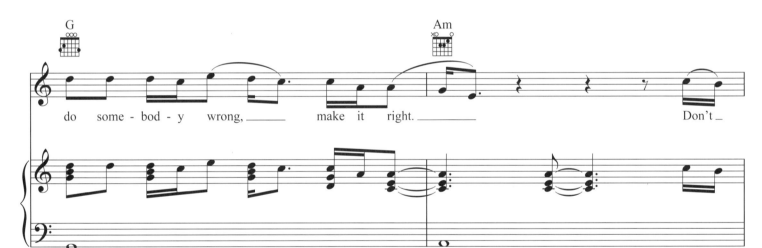

do some-bod-y wrong, _____ make it right. _____ Don't _

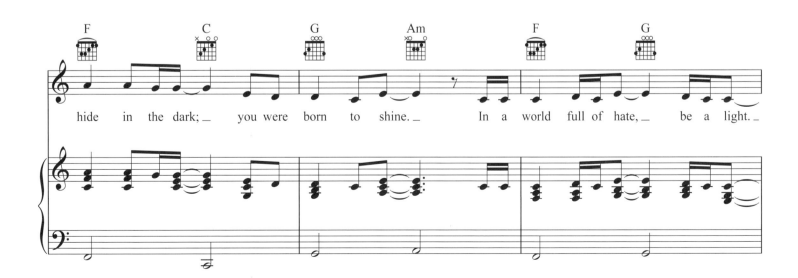

hide in the dark; _ you were born to shine. _ In a world full of hate, _ be a light. _

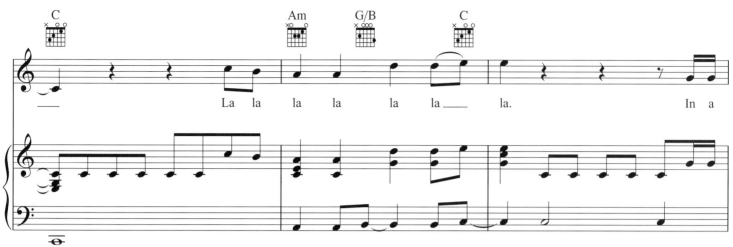

La la la la la la la. In a

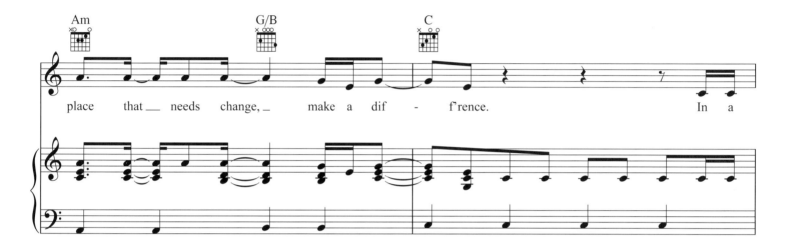

place that ___ needs change, ___ make a dif - f'rence. In a

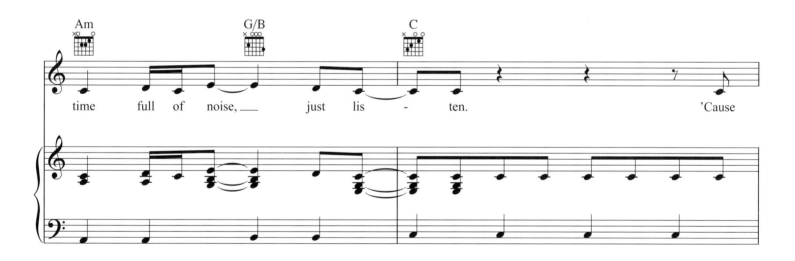

time full of noise, ___ just lis - ten. 'Cause

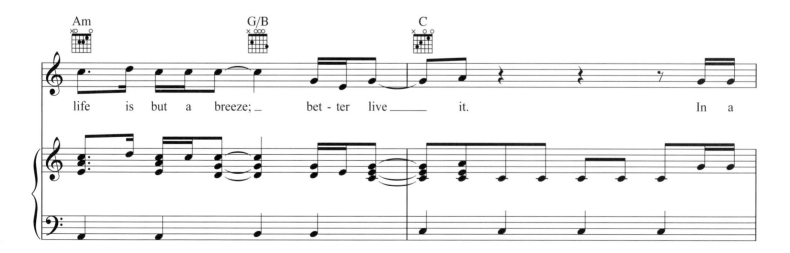

life is but a breeze; ___ bet - ter live _____ it. In a

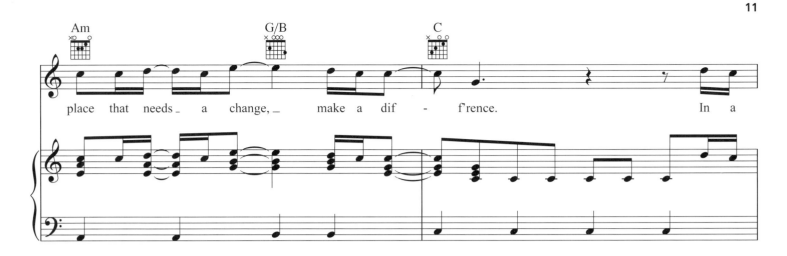

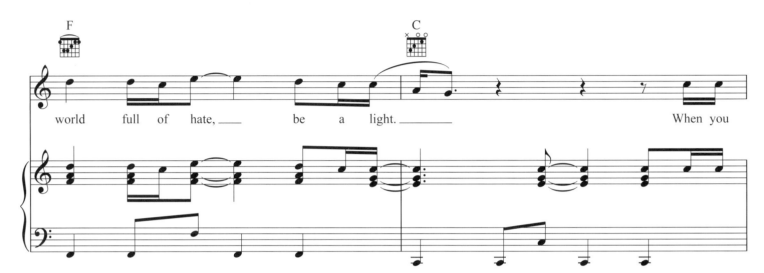

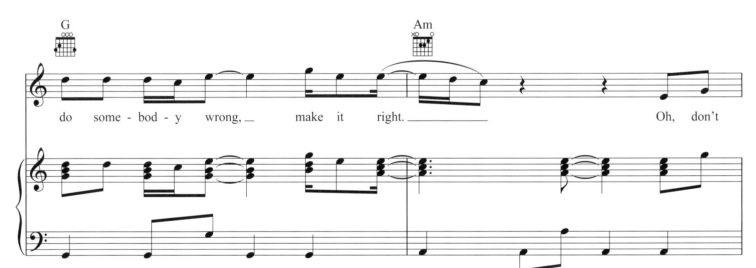

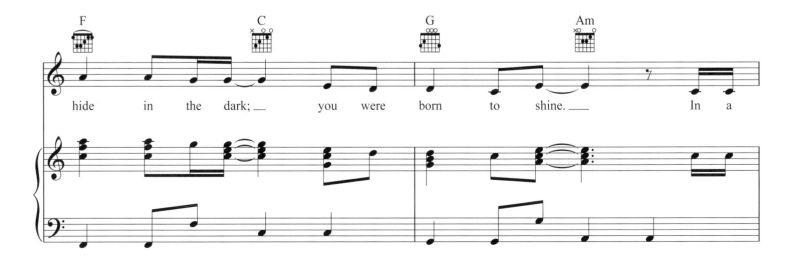

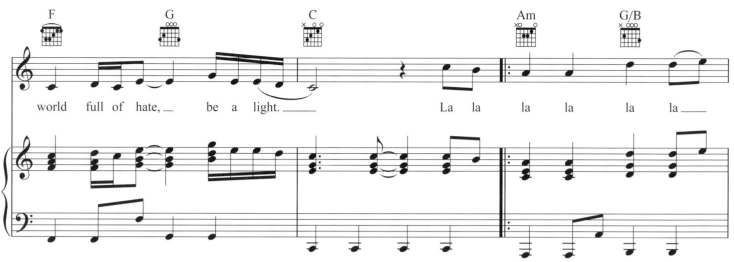

world full of hate, __ be a light. ____ La la la la la la ____

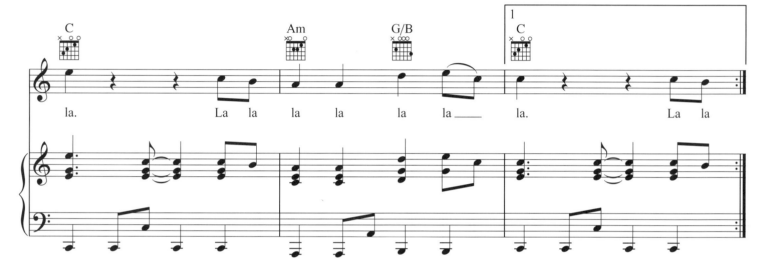

la. La la la la la la ____ la. La la

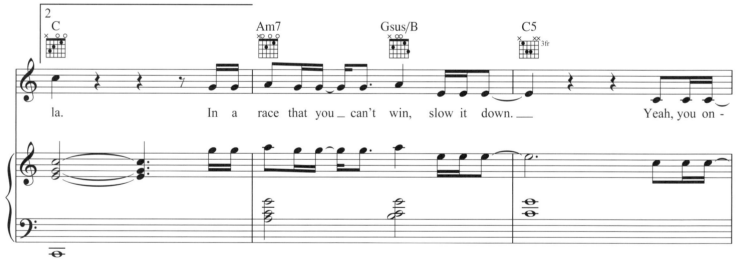

la. In a race that you __ can't win, slow it down. __ Yeah, you on -

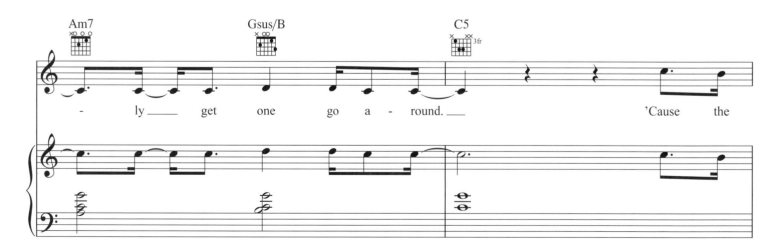

- ly ____ get one go a - round. __ 'Cause the

finish line — is six — feet in the ground. — In a

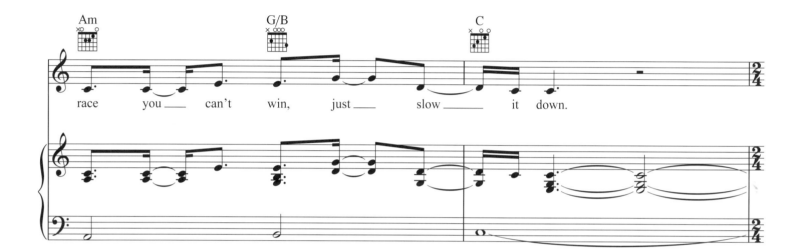

race you — can't win, just — slow — it down.

In a world full of hate, — be a light. —

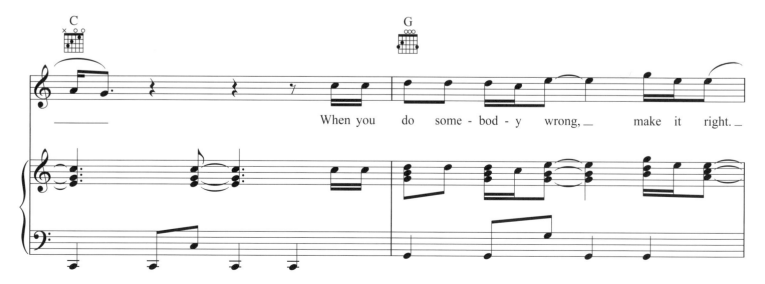

— When you do some-bod-y wrong, — make it right. —

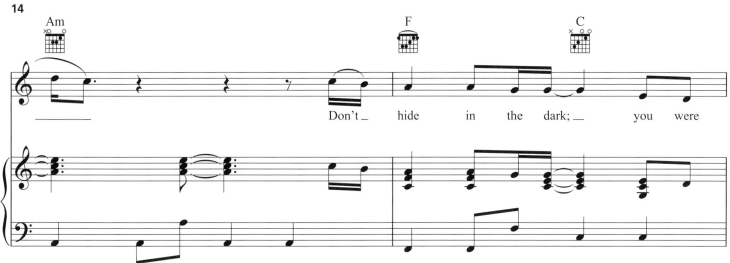

BETTER THAN TODAY

Words and Music by RHYS LEWIS
and AIDAN GLOVER

Moderate Ballad

I don't read the head - lines and I don't watch the news, __ 'cause I lose faith __ in some - thing ev - 'ry time __ I do. Well, I don't need to bur - y my head in __ the sand, __ but

I'm just tryin' to live __ this life __ as best __ as I __ can.

Times __ get tough, but I don't __ give up, 'cause I know __ I'm not a - lone. __

__ 'Cause we're all reach - ing for some - thing, __ we're all crav -

- ing __ change, __ hop - ing to - mor - row, to - mor - row is bet -

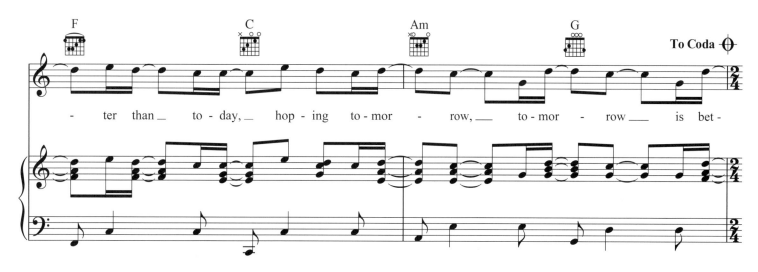

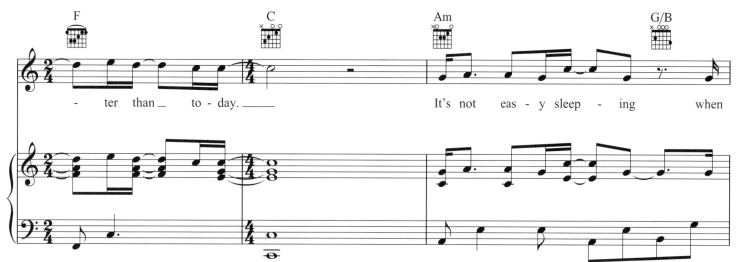

I lay down in bed, __ 'cause I got all __ these wor - ries run - ning through __

__ my head. __ And it's hard __ to keep push - ing for - ward when

trou - ble pulls __ you back, __ and you wake __ up e - ven fur - ther from __ a dream __

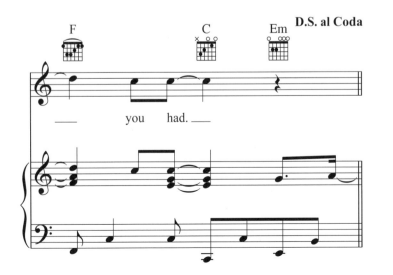

__ you had. __

D.S. al Coda

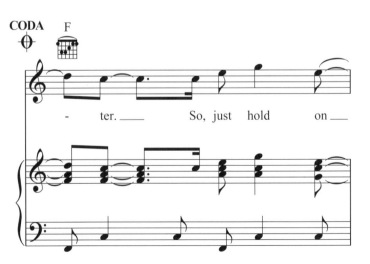

CODA

- ter. __ So, just hold on __

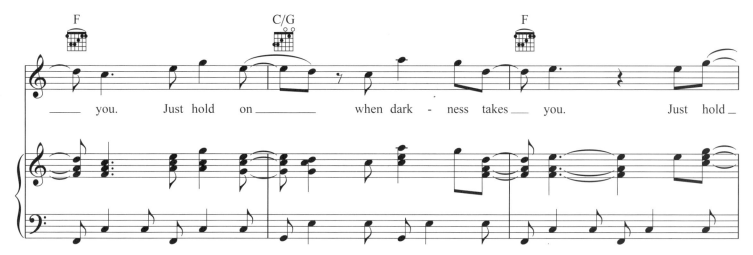

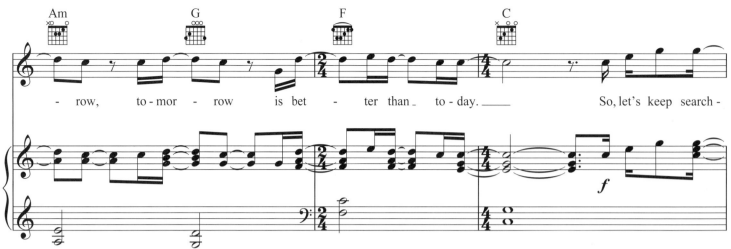

- row, to-mor-row is bet - ter than _ to - day. _____ So, let's keep search-

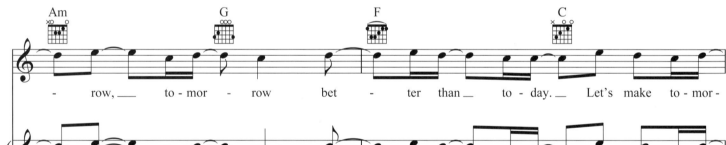

- ing for some - where; _ we're gon-na find ___ a way _ to make to-mor-

- row, ___ to - mor - row bet - ter than _ to - day. _ Let's make to-mor-

- row, ___ to - mor - row bet - ter than _ to - day. _ Let's make to-mor-

- row, ___ to - mor - row bet - ter than __ to - day. __ Let's make to - mor -

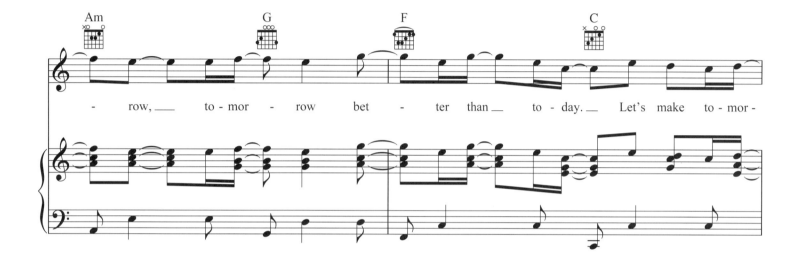

- row, ___ to - mor - row bet - ter than __ to - day. __ Let's make to - mor -

- row, ___ to - mor - row bet - ter than __ to - day. __ Let's make to - mor -

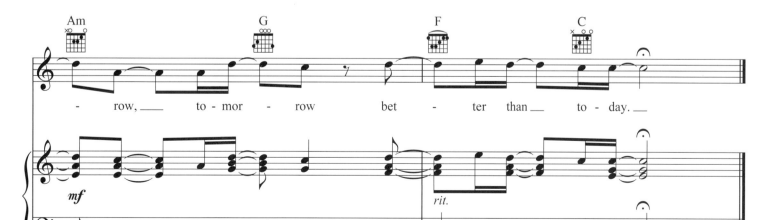

- row, ___ to - mor - row bet - ter than __ to - day. __

BETTER DAYS

Words and Music by RYAN TEDDER,
BRENT KUTZLE and JOHN NATHANIEL

Oh, I know that there'll be bet - ter days. ___

Oh, that sun-shine 'bout to come my way. ___ May we nev-er, ev-er shed an - oth - er

tear for to - day, ___ 'cause, oh, I know that there'll be bet - ter days. ___ Wak-ing

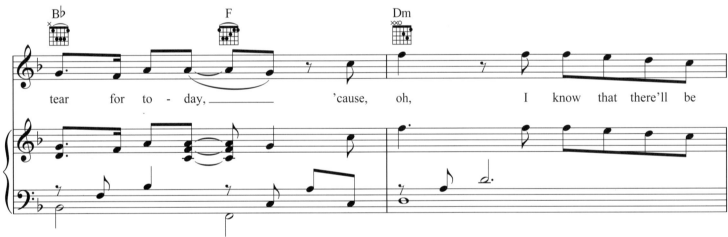

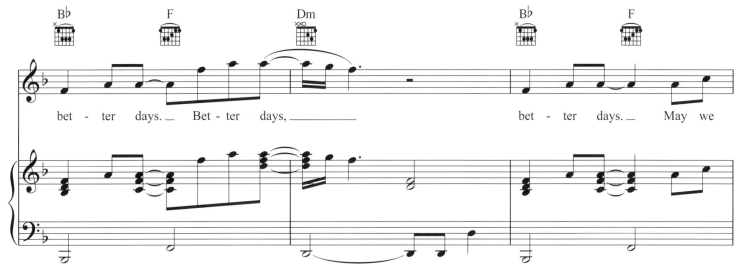

bet - ter days. __ Bet - ter days, _____ bet - ter days. __ May we

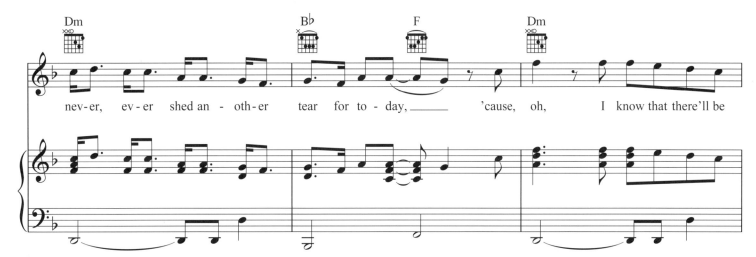

nev - er, ev - er shed an - oth - er tear for to - day, _____ 'cause, oh, I know that there'll be

bet - ter days. ____ May we nev - er, ev - er shed an - oth - er

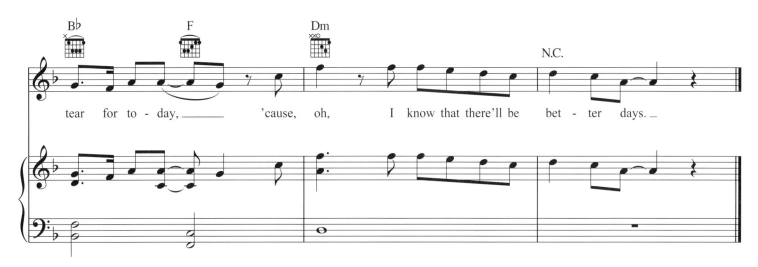

tear for to - day, _____ 'cause, oh, I know that there'll be bet - ter days. __

CHANGE

Words and Music by CHARLIE PUTH,
JENS CARLSSON and ROSS GOLAN

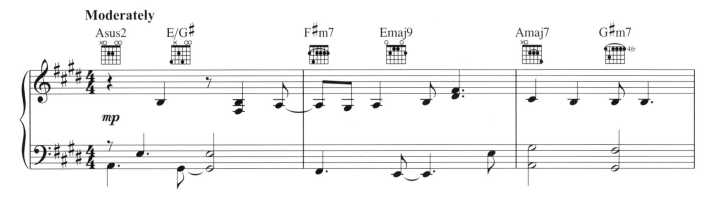

Why are we look-ing down on our
Look a-round; there are too man-y
What a waste it would be to de-

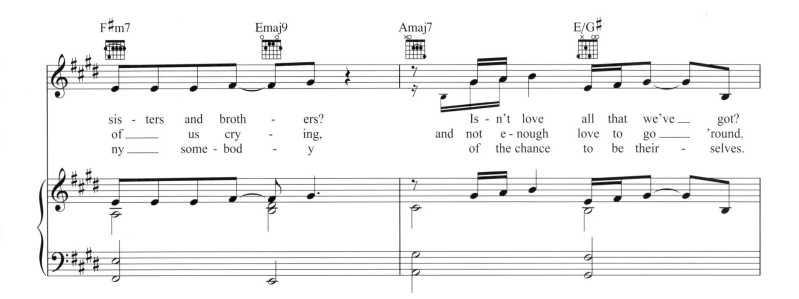

sis-ters and broth-ers? Is-n't love all that we've__ got?
of__ us cry-ing, and not e-nough love to go__ 'round.
ny__ some-bod-y of the chance to be their-selves.

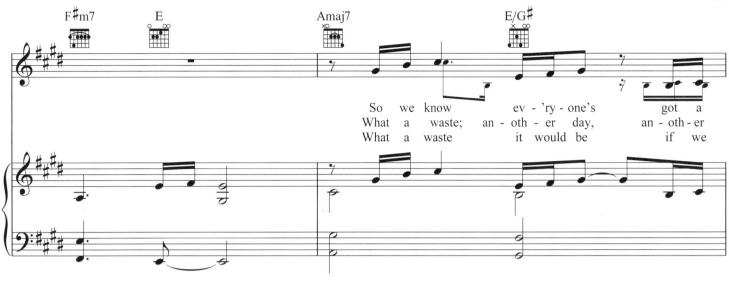

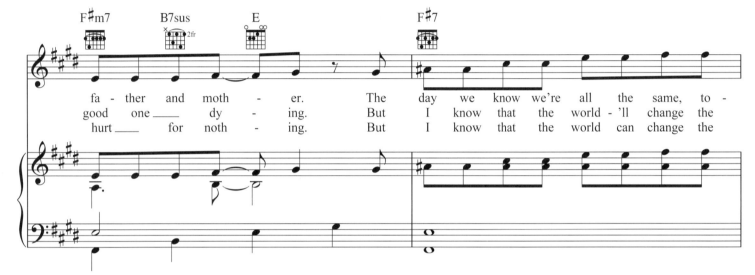

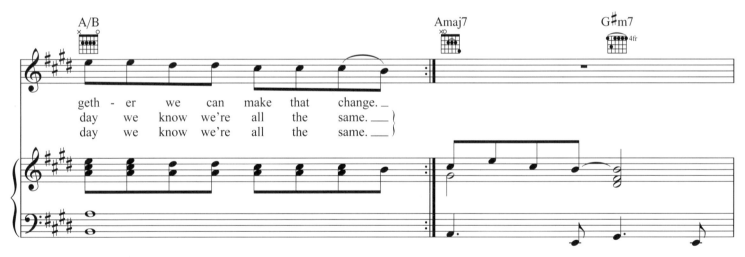

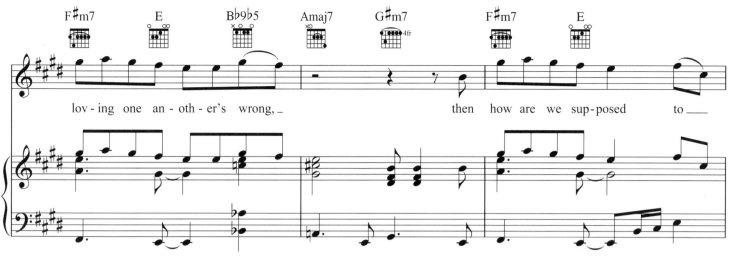

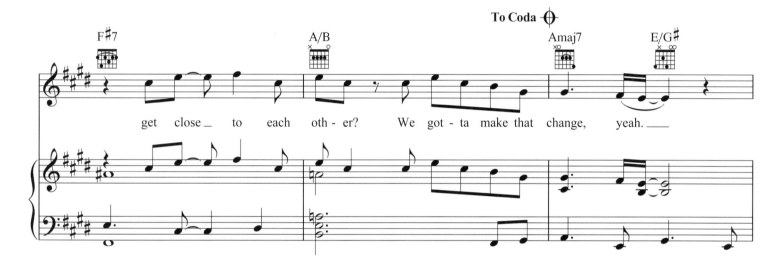

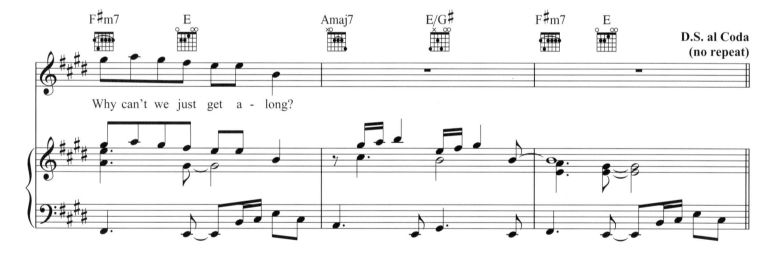

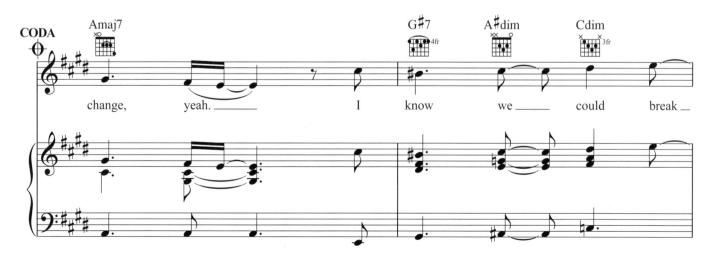

CROWDED TABLE

Words and Music by NATALIE HEMBY,
LORI McKENNA and BRANDI CARLILE

Recorded a half step lower.

street - light show - ing you the way home, _____ if you can hold

my hand when you need to let go.

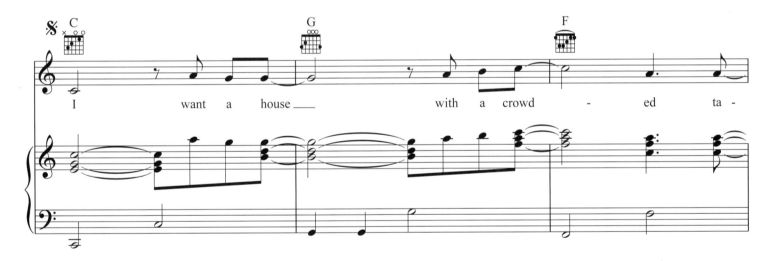

I want a house ____ with a crowd - ed ta -

- ble, and a place ____ by the fire ____ for ____

ev - 'ry - one. ____ Let us take ____ on the world ____

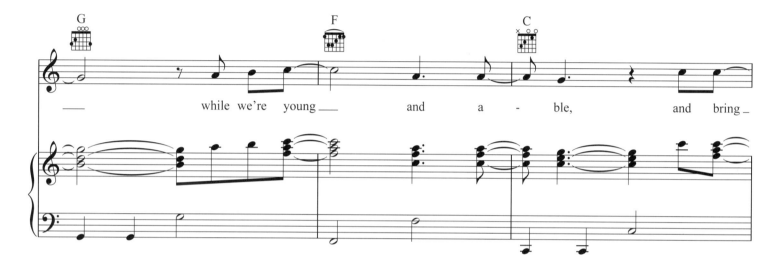

____ while we're young ____ and a - ble, and bring ____

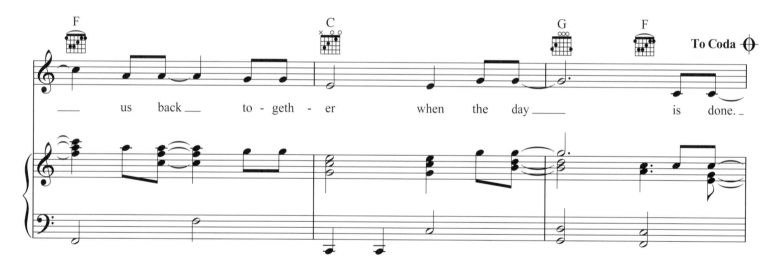

____ us back ____ to - geth - er when the day ____ is done. ____

To Coda

____ If we want a gar - den, we're gon - na have to

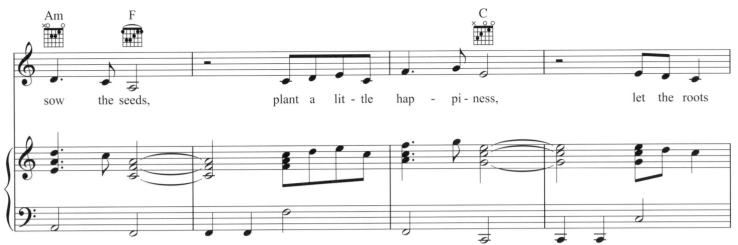

sow the seeds, plant a lit- tle hap - pi - ness, let the roots

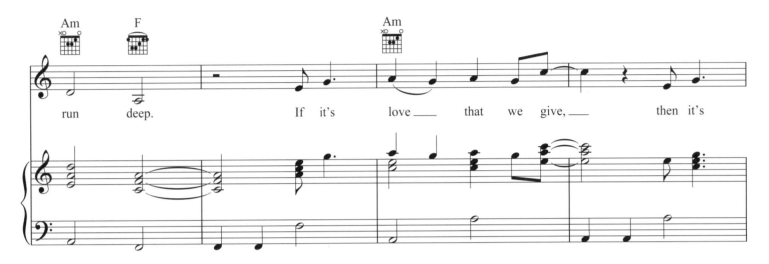

run deep. If it's love ___ that we give, ___ then it's

love ___ that we reap. ___ If we want a gar - den,

D.S. al Coda

we're gon - na have to sow the seeds, yeah. ___

CODA

The door is al - ways o - pen, ___ your

pic - ture's on ___ my ___ wall. ___ Ev - 'ry - one's a lit - tle bro -

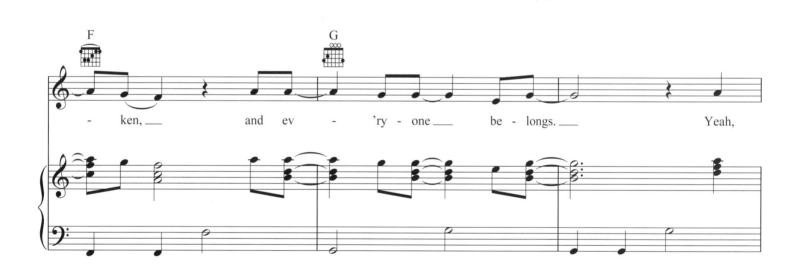

- ken, ___ and ev - 'ry - one ___ be - longs. ___ Yeah,

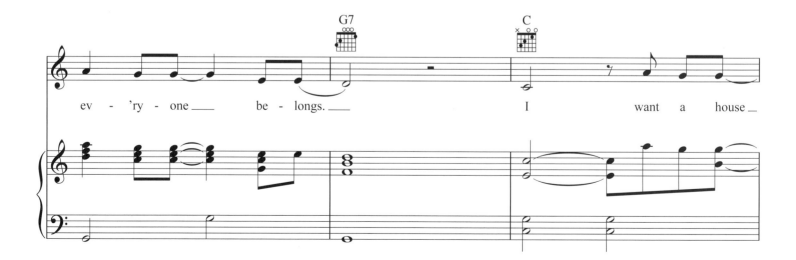

ev - 'ry - one ___ be - longs. ___ I want a house ___

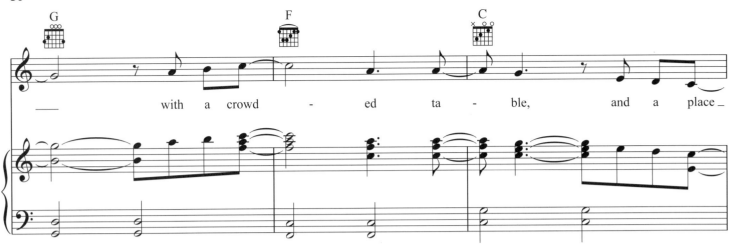

with a crowd - ed ta - ble, and a place __

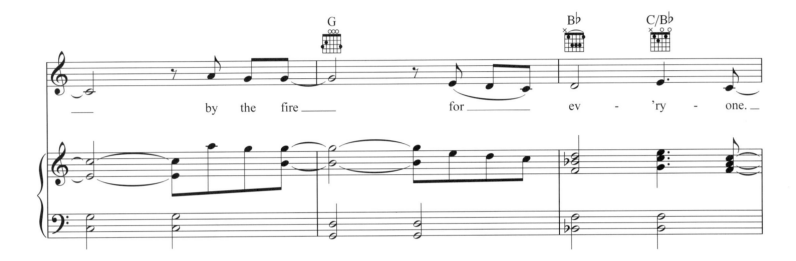

__ by the fire __ for __ ev - 'ry - one. __

__ Let us take __ on the world __ while we're young __

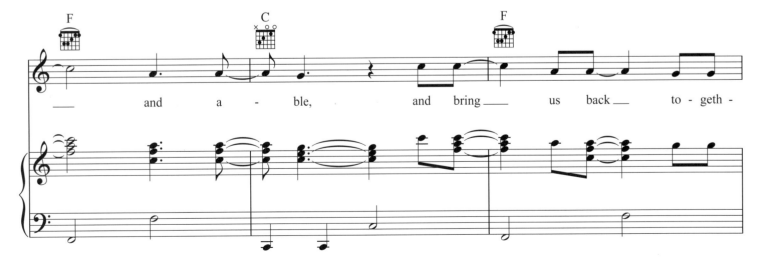

__ and a - ble, and bring __ us back __ to - geth -

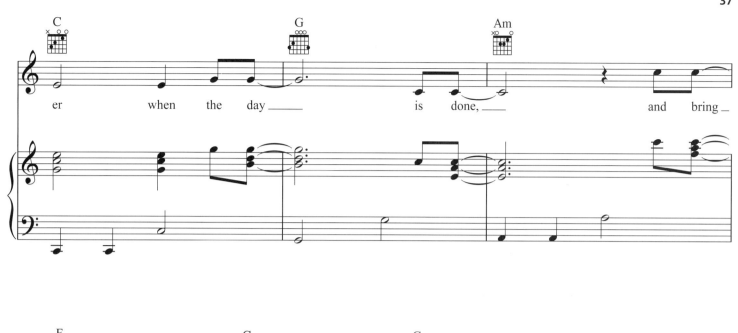

er when the day ____ is done, ____ and bring __

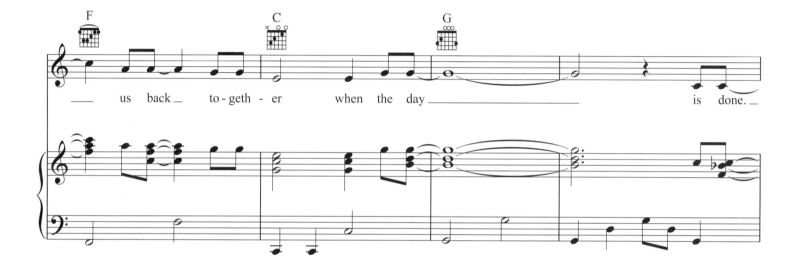

__ us back __ to - geth - er when the day _____ is done. __

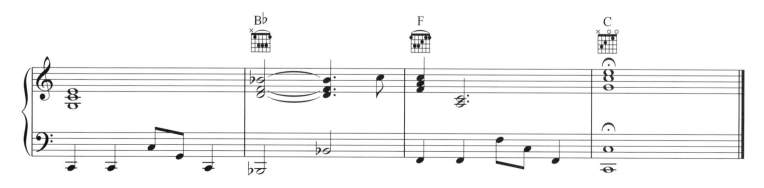

COUNT ON ME

Words and Music by BRUNO MARS,
ARI LEVINE and PHILIP LAWRENCE

Moderately fast

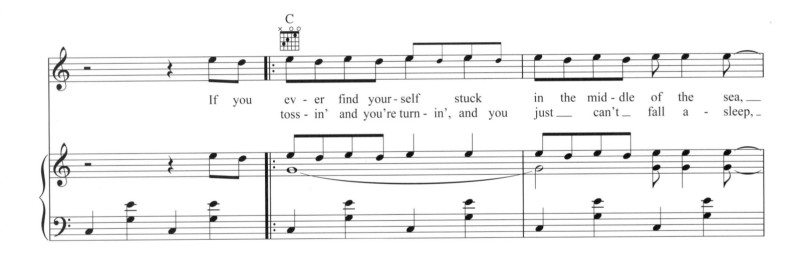

to find _____ you. _____
be - side _____ you. _____ If you
And if you

ev - er find your-self lost in the dark, and you can't see, _____
ev - er for - get how much you real - ly mean to me, _____

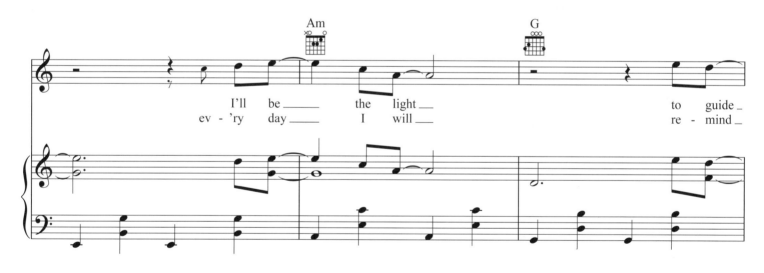

I'll be _____ the light _____ to guide _____
ev - 'ry day _____ I will _____ re - mind _____

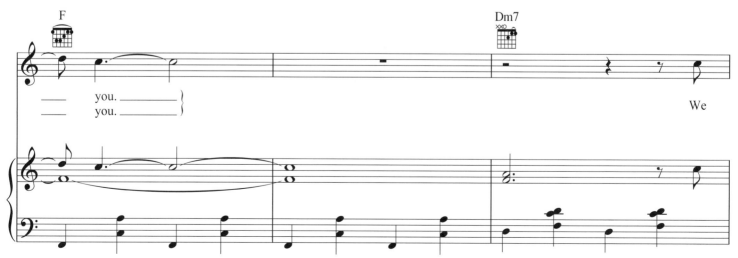

_____ you. _____
_____ you. _____
We

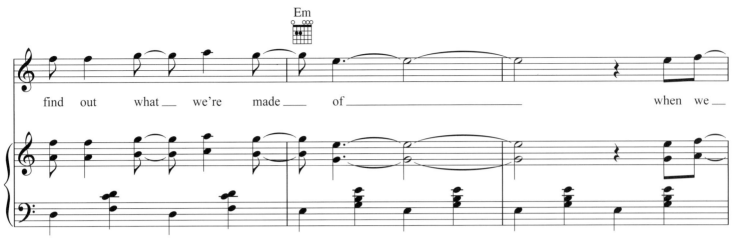

find out what __ we're made __ of _____ when we __

__ are called __ to help __ our friends _ in need. __

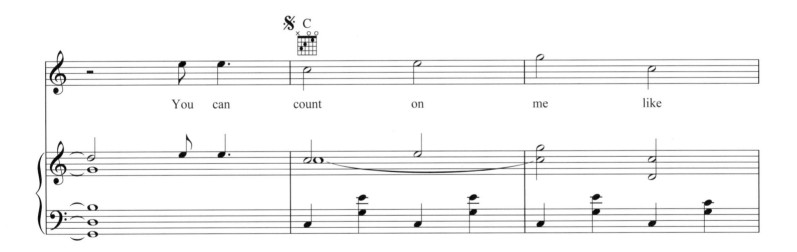

You can count on me like

"one, two, three." I'll be _____ there,

and I know when I need it. I can

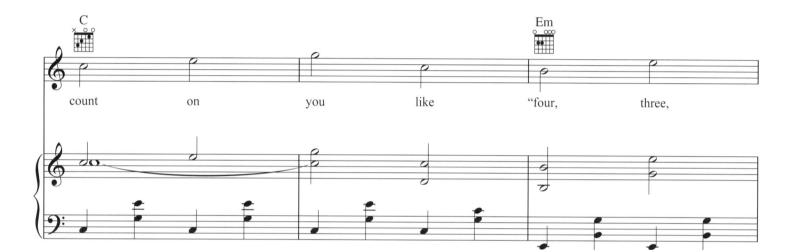

count on you like "four, three,

two," and you'll be _____ there, 'cause that's _

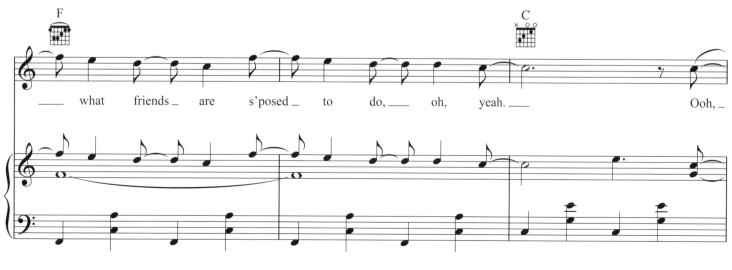

_ what friends _ are s'posed _ to do, ___ oh, yeah. ___ Ooh, _

EBONY AND IVORY

Words and Music by
PAUL McCARTNEY

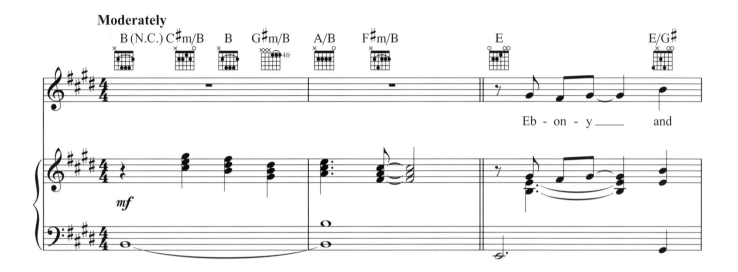

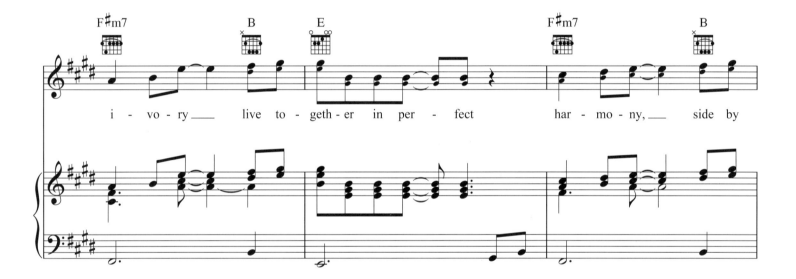

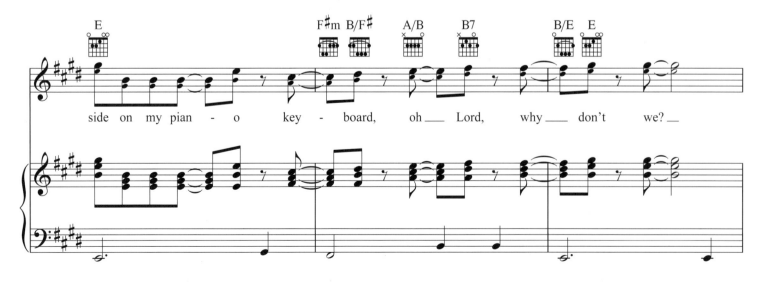

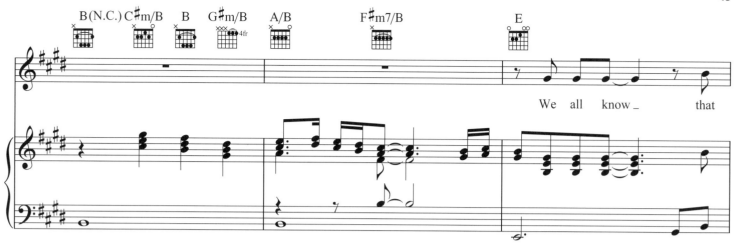

We all know _ that

peo - ple are the same wher - ev - er you go. _ There is good and bad in ev-

- 'ry - one. _ We learn to live _ { we / when we } learn to give each oth - er what we need _

___ to sur - vive, _ to - geth - er a - live. _____ Eb - on - y ____ and

i - vo - ry ___ live to - geth - er in per - fect har - mo - ny, ___ side by

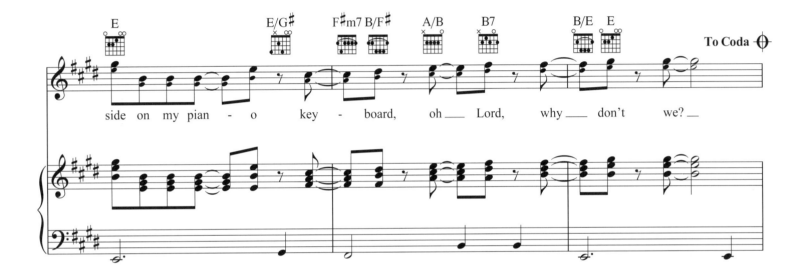

side on my pian - o key - board, oh ___ Lord, why ___ don't we? ___

To Coda

Double tempo

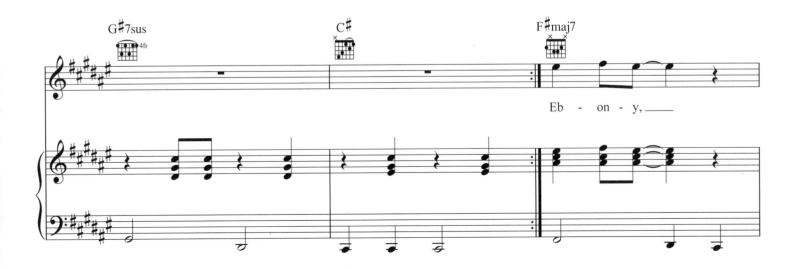

Eb - on - y, ___

Double tempo

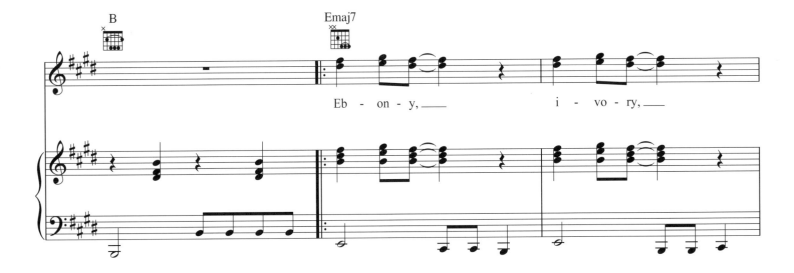

Eb - on - y, _____ i - vo - ry, _____

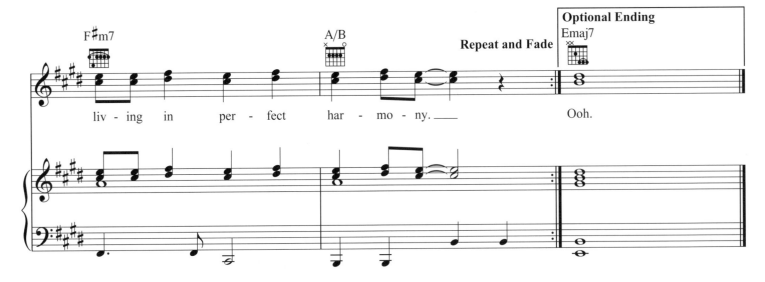

liv - ing in per - fect har - mo - ny. _____ Ooh.

FROM A DISTANCE

Words and Music by
JULIE GOLD

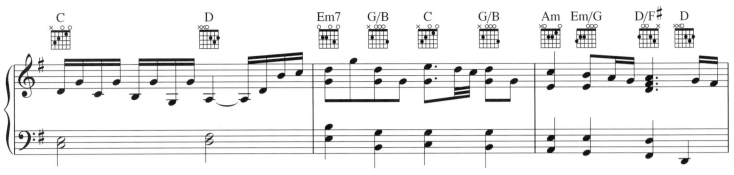

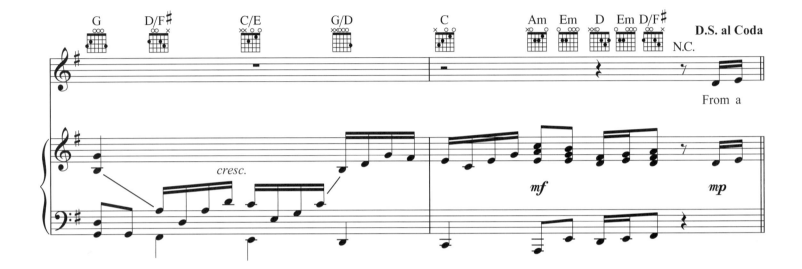

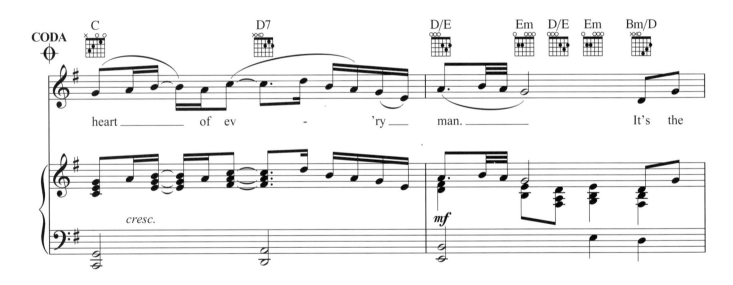

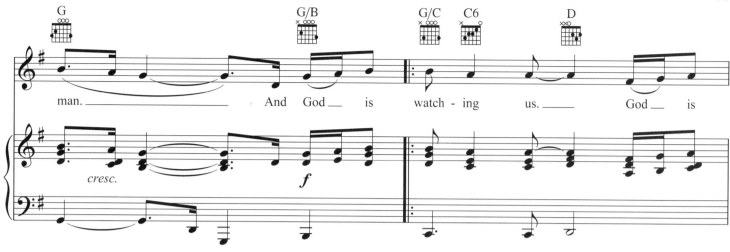

man. _____ And God ___ is watch-ing us. _____ God ___ is

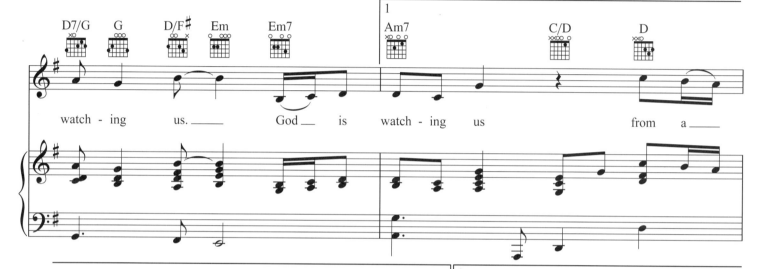

watch-ing us. _____ God ___ is watch-ing us from a _____

dis-tance. _____ Oh, God is _____ watch-ing us _____ from a

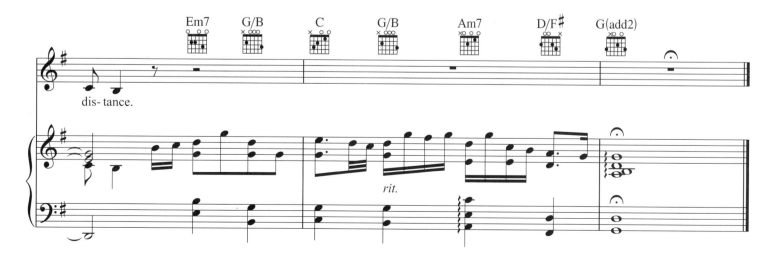

dis-tance.

EVERYBODY HURTS

Words and Music by WILLIAM BERRY,
PETER BUCK, MICHAEL MILLS
and MICHAEL STIPE

nough
much
much

of this life, ___
of this life, ___
of this life ___

well, hang on. ___
well, hang on ___
to hang on. ___

___
___
___

Don't let your - self   go,
'cause ev - 'ry - bod - y   hurts.
Well, ev - 'ry - bod - y   hurts   some-

ev - 'ry - bod - y   cries
Take com - fort ___ in your   friends.
times,   ev - 'ry - bod - y   cries.

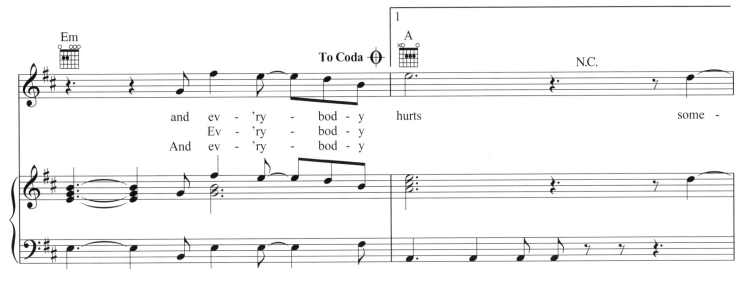

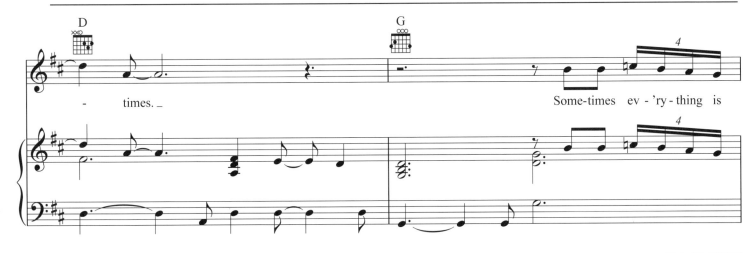

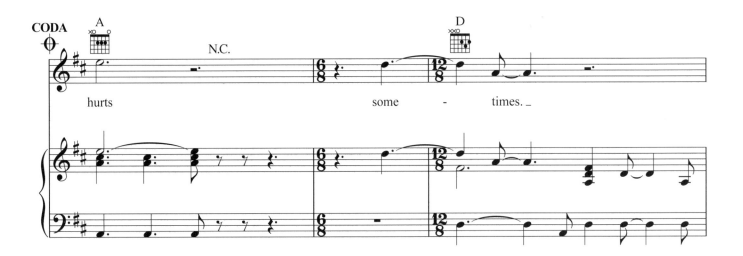

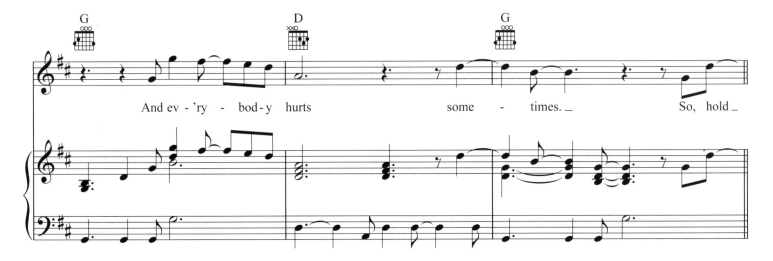

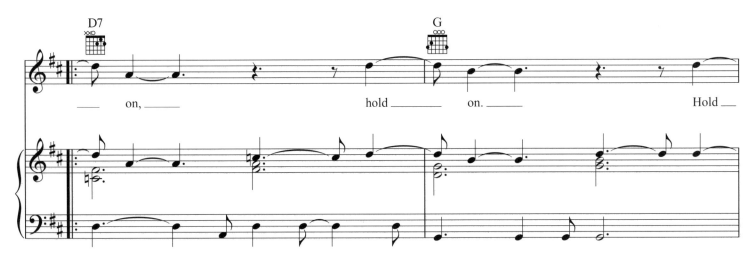

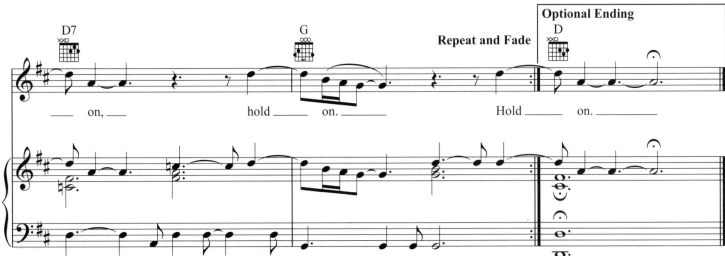

GOOD JOB

Words and Music by ALICIA AUGELLO-COOK,
KASSEEM DEAN, AVERY CHAMBLISS
and TERIUS NASH

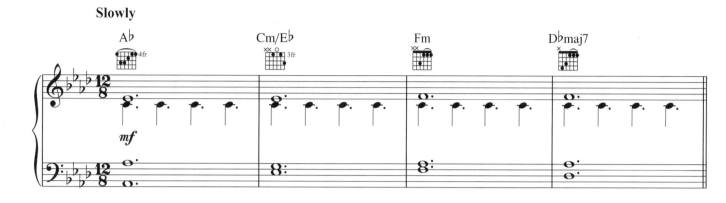

You're the en - gine that makes all things go; and you're al - ways in dis - guise, my he -

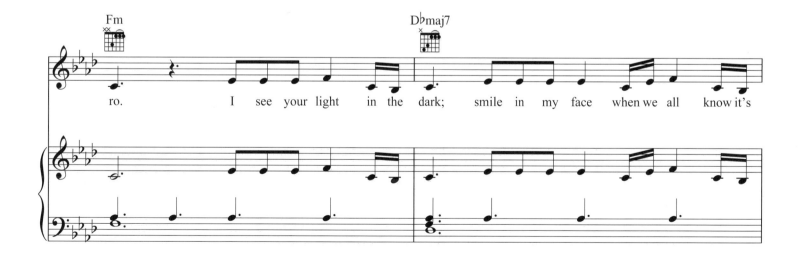

ro. I see your light in the dark; smile in my face when we all know it's

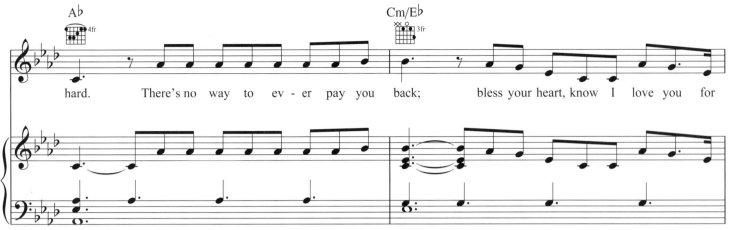

hard. There's no way to ev-er pay you back; bless your heart, know I love you for

that. Hon-est and self-less. I don't know if this helps it, ___ but,

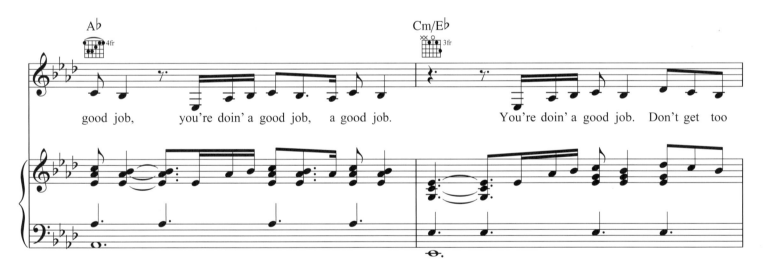

good job, you're doin' a good job, a good job. You're doin' a good job. Don't get too

down, _ the world needs you now. _ Know that you mat-ter, ___ mat-ter, ___ mat-ter, ___ yeah. ___

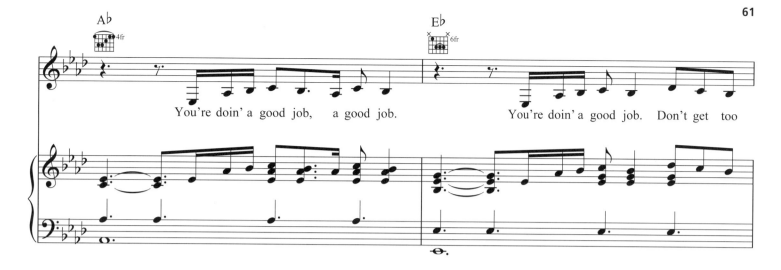

You're doin' a good job, a good job. You're doin' a good job. Don't get too

down, _ the world needs you now. _ Know that you mat-ter, _ mat-ter, _ mat-ter, _ yeah. _

Six in the morn - ing... as soon as you walk through that door, ev-'ry-one needs you a -

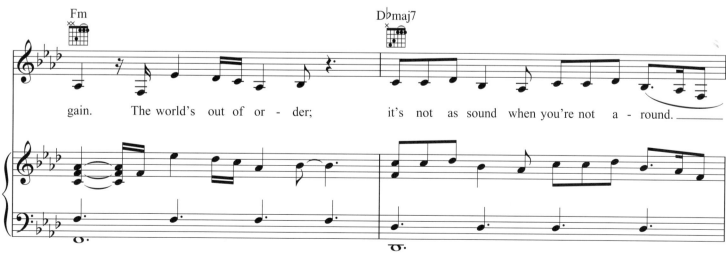

gain. The world's out of or - der; it's not as sound when you're not a - round. _

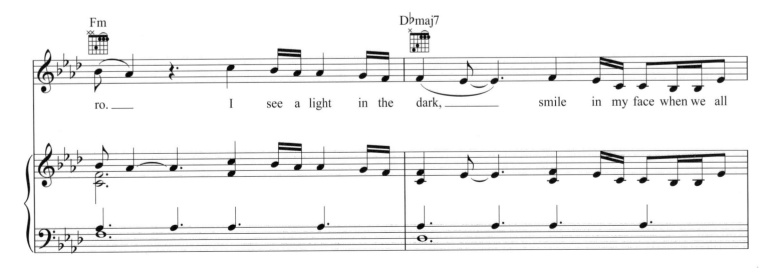

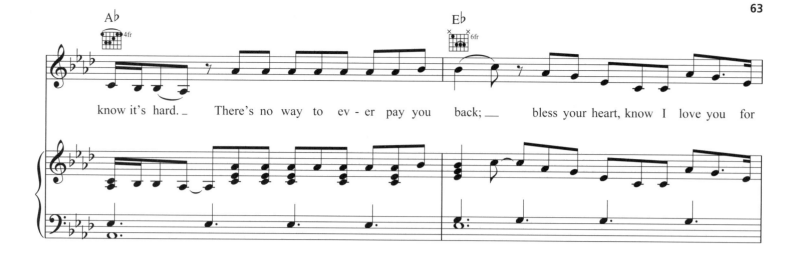

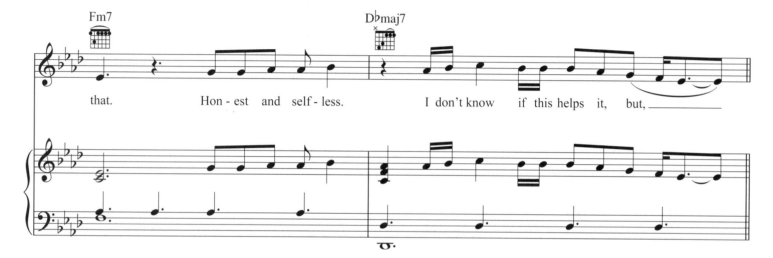

You're doin' a good job, a good job. You're doin' a good job. Don't get too

down, the world needs you now. Know that you mat-ter, mat-ter, mat-ter, yeah.

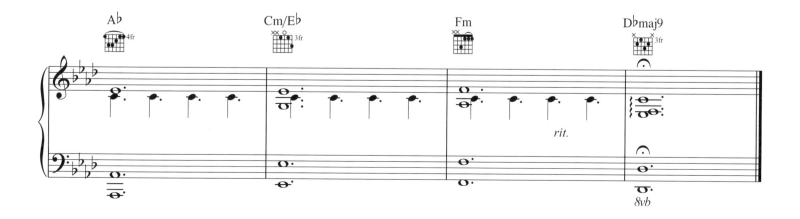

FIGHT SONG

Words and Music by RACHEL PLATTEN
and DAVE BASSETT

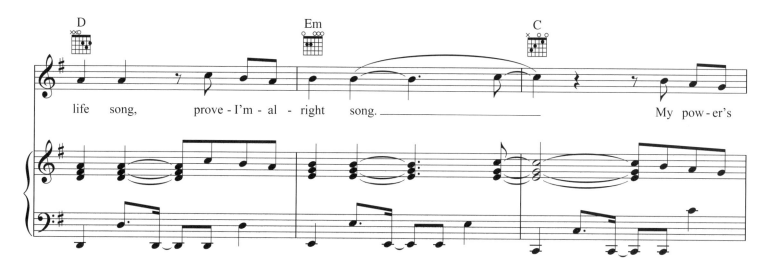

turned on. Start-ing right now __ I'll be strong. I'll play my fight song. And I

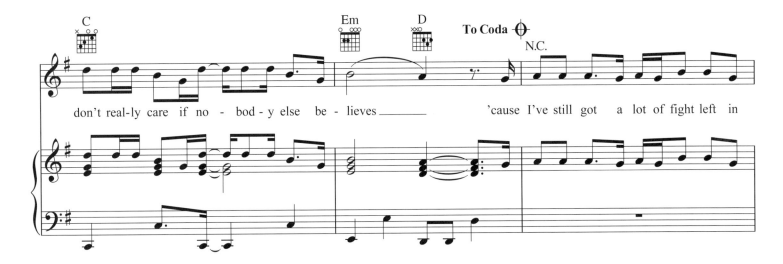

don't real-ly care if no - bod - y else be - lieves _____ 'cause I've still got a lot of fight left in

me. Los - in' friends __ and I'm __ chas - in' sleep.

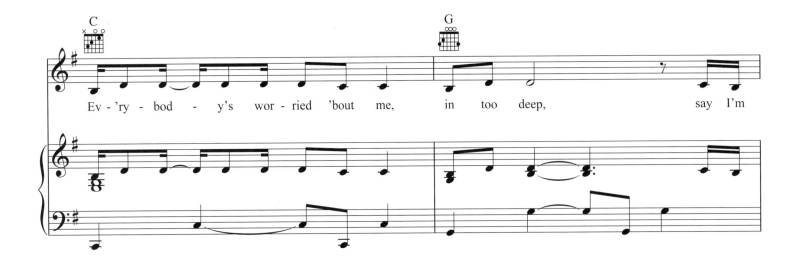

Ev - 'ry - bod — y's wor - ried 'bout me, in too deep, say I'm

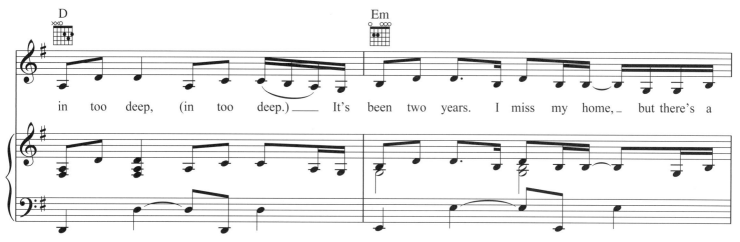

in too deep, (in too deep.) It's been two years. I miss my home, but there's a

fire burn - in' in my bones. I still be - lieve, yeah, I

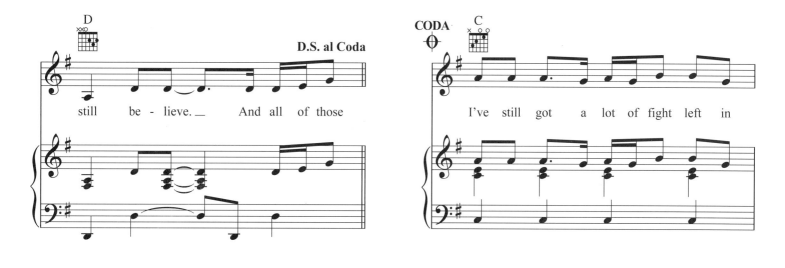

D.S. al Coda

CODA

still be - lieve. And all of those

I've still got a lot of fight left in

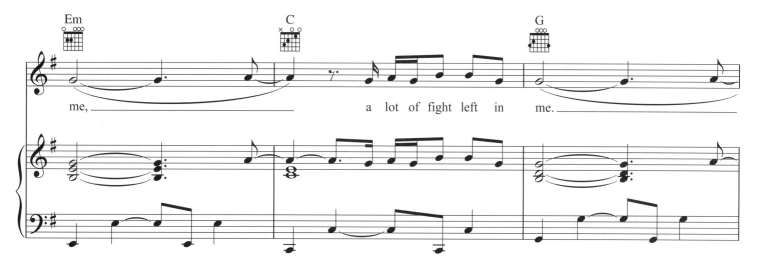

me, a lot of fight left in me.

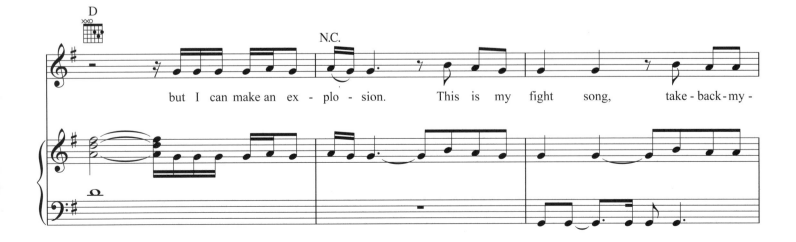

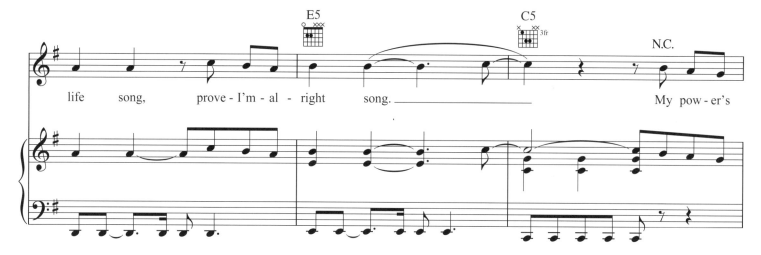

life song, prove-I'm-al-right song. _____ My pow-er's

turned on. Start-ing right now _ I'll be strong. I'll play my fight song. And I

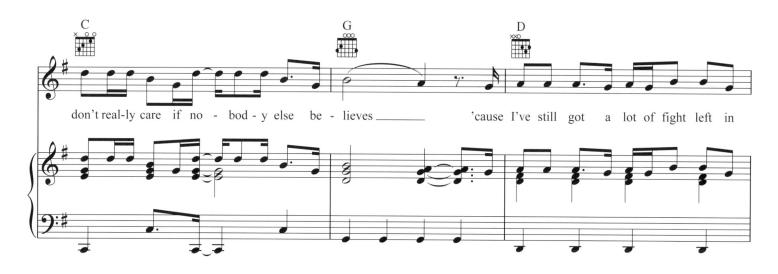

don't real-ly care if no-bod-y else be-lieves _____ 'cause I've still got a lot of fight left in

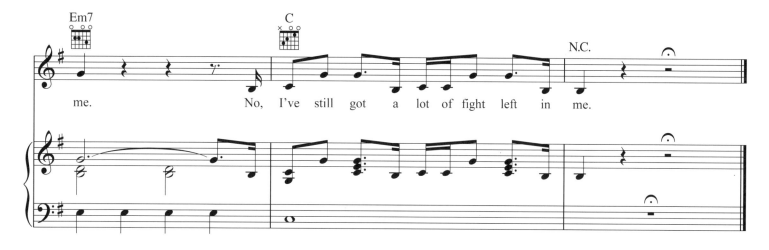

me. No, I've still got a lot of fight left in me.

I DARE YOU

Words and Music by BENJAMIN WEST,
JEFFREY GITELMAN, NATALIE HEMBY,
LAURA VELTZ and JESSE SHATKIN

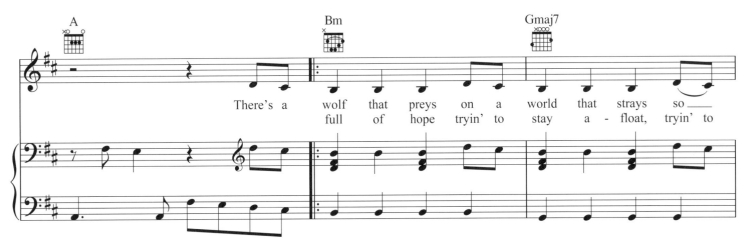

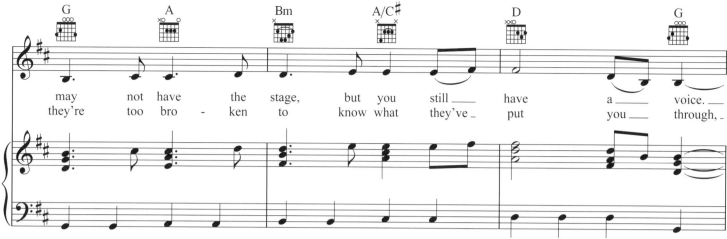

may not have the stage, but you still ___ have a ___ voice. ___
they're too bro - ken to know what still they've _ put you ___ through, _

You may not have the strength, but if you ___
do the on - ly thing that you'd want ___

have a ___ choice, ___
done to ___ you. ___ Oh, _____ I

dare you to love. ___
Oh, _____

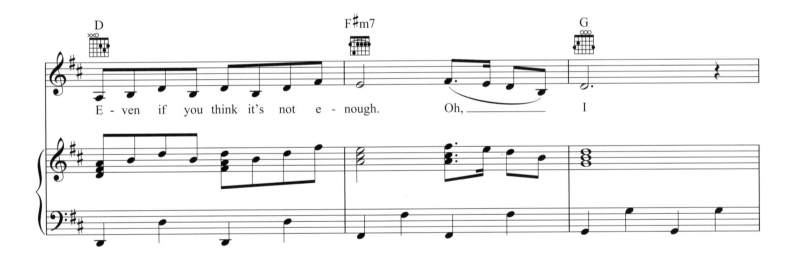

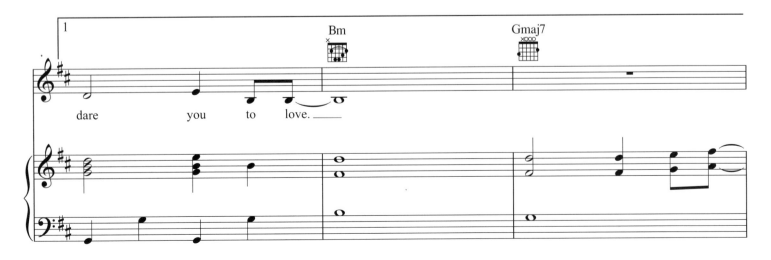

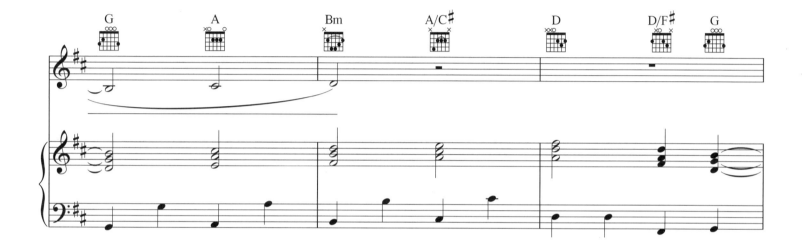

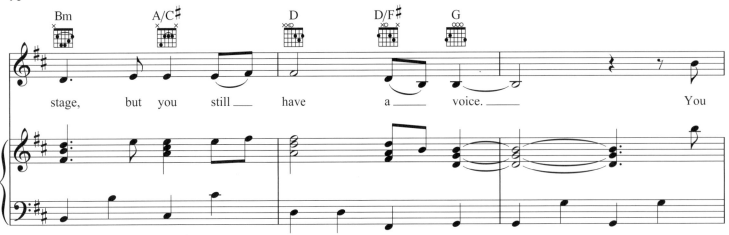

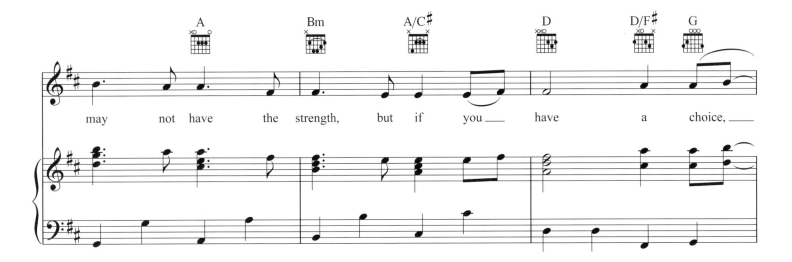

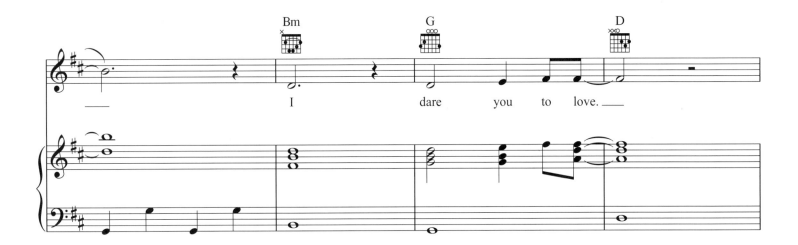

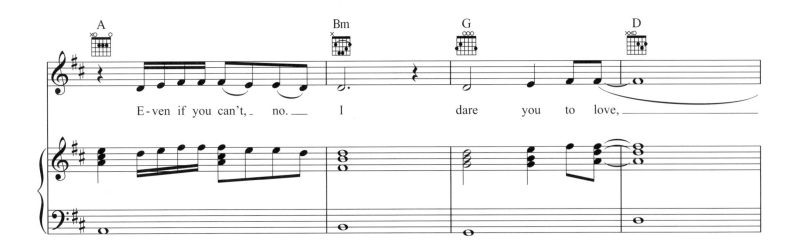

oh. E - ven if you're hurt and you can on - ly ___ see the worst.

E - ven if you think it's not e - nough. Oh, _____ I, I

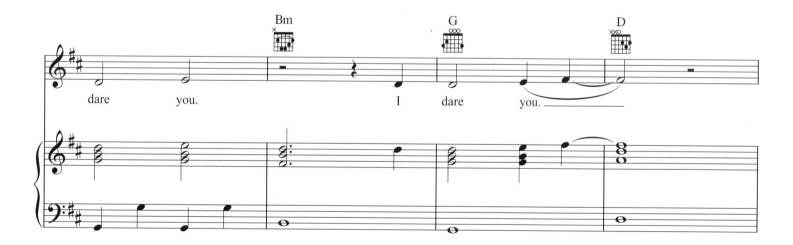

dare you. I dare you. _____

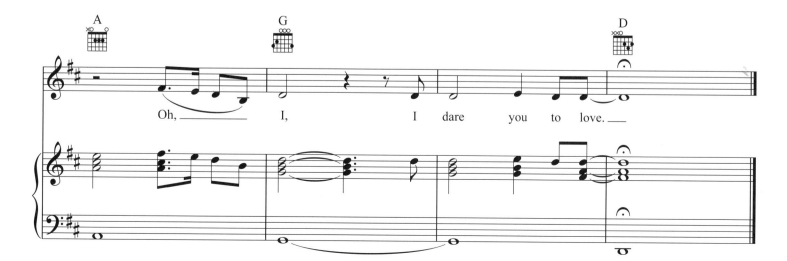

Oh, _____ I, I dare you to love. ___

I WON'T LET GO

Words and Music by JASON SELLERS
and STEVE ROBSON

Slow Gospel Ballad

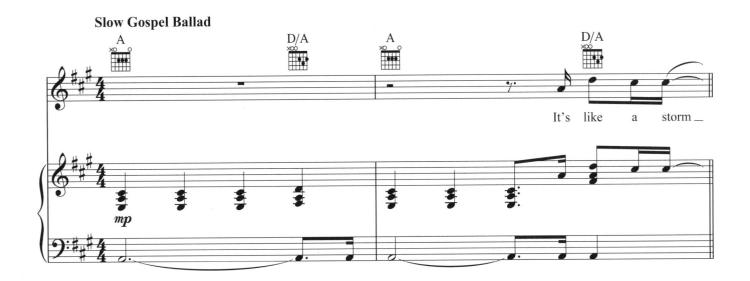

It's like a storm

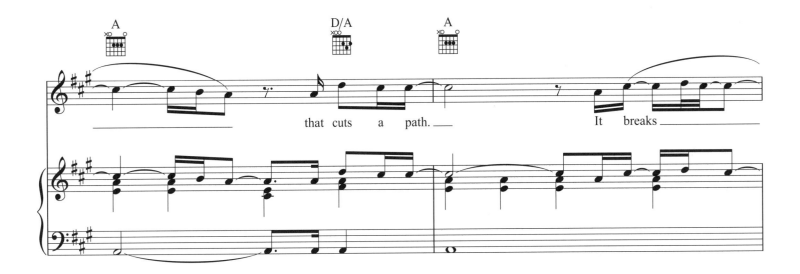

that cuts a path. It breaks

your will, it feels like that. You think you're lost;

but you're not lost, on your

own. You're not a-lone. I will

stand by you. I will help you through when you've

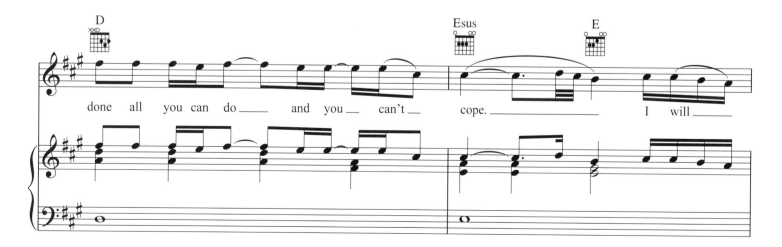

done all you can do and you can't cope. I will

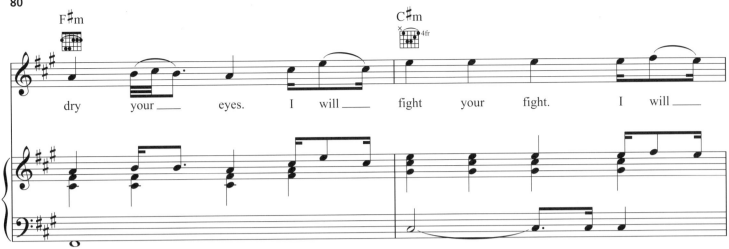

dry your ___ eyes. I will ___ fight your fight. I will ___

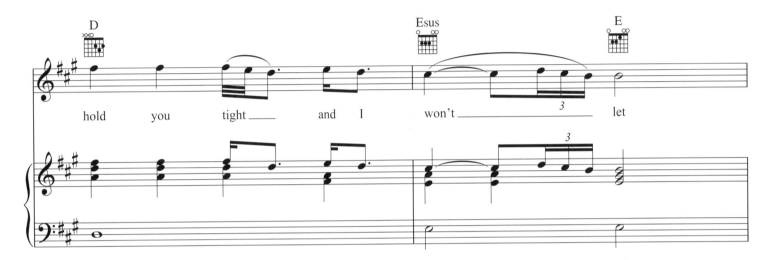

hold you tight ___ and I won't _____ let

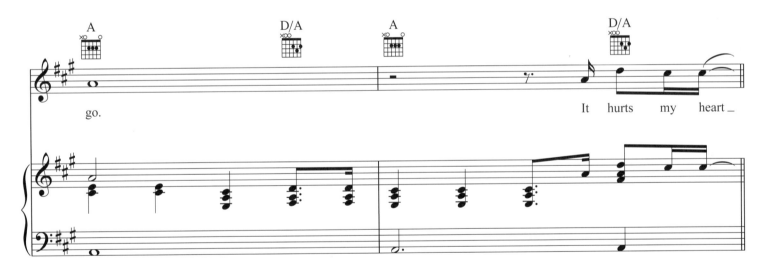

go. It hurts my heart _

___ to see you cry. ___ I know _____

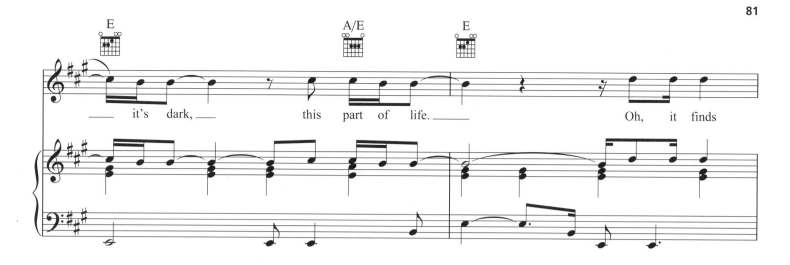

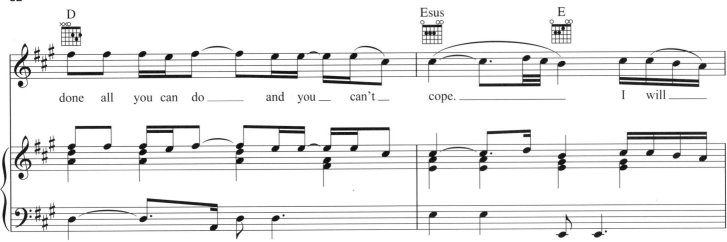

done all you can do _____ and you _____ can't _____ cope. _____ I will _____

dry your eyes. I will _____ fight your fight. I will _____ hold you tight _____ and I

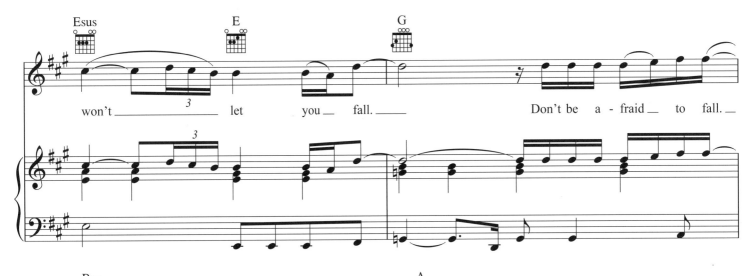

won't _____ let you _____ fall. _____ Don't be a - fraid _____ to fall. _____

_____ I'm right here _____ to catch _____ you. _____ I won't let you _____ down. _____

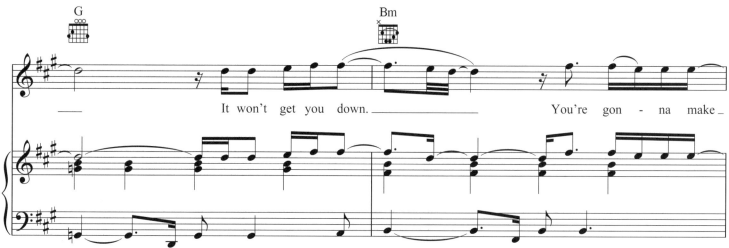

It won't get you down. _____ You're gon - na make _

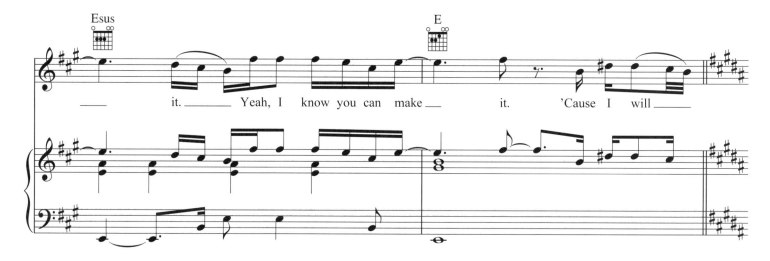

_____ it. ____ Yeah, I know you can make ___ it. 'Cause I will _____

stand by you. I will _ help you through when you've _ done all you can do and you _ can't _

cope. _____ And I will dry _____ your _____ eyes. I will _

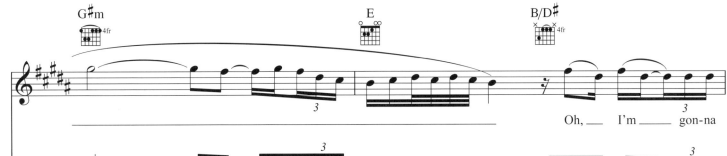

HEAL THE WORLD

Words and Music by
MICHAEL JACKSON

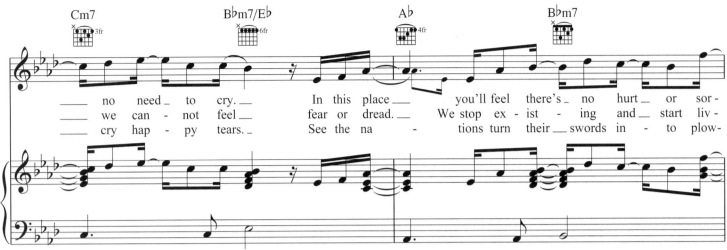

you and — for me — and — the en - tire hu - man race. — There are

peo - ple dy - ing; if you care e - nough — for the liv - ing, make a

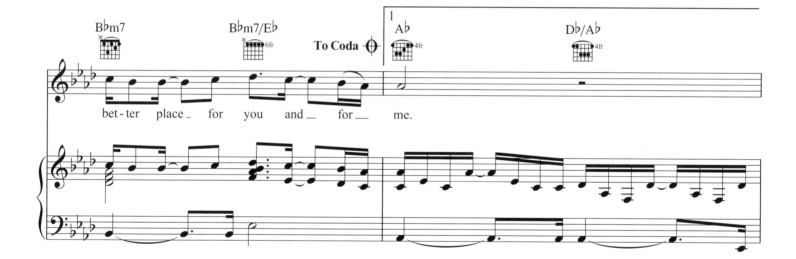

bet - ter place — for you and — for — me.

If you want — me.

And the

dream we were_ con - ceived_ in will_ re - veal a joy - ful face._ And the

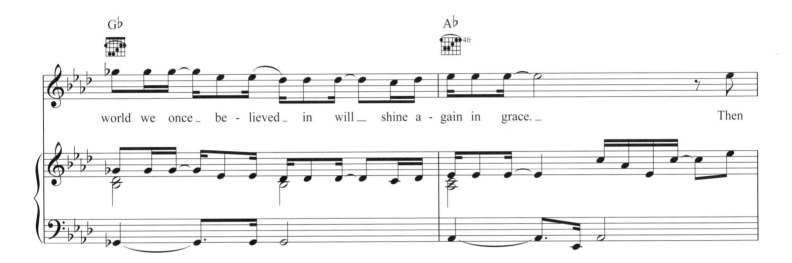

world we once_ be - lieved_ in will_ shine a - gain in grace._ Then

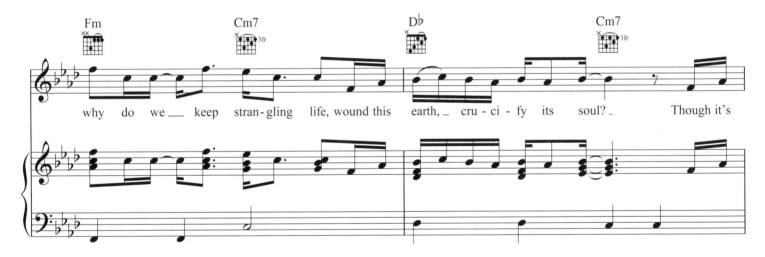

why do we __ keep stran - gling life, wound this earth, _ cru - ci - fy its soul? _ Though it's

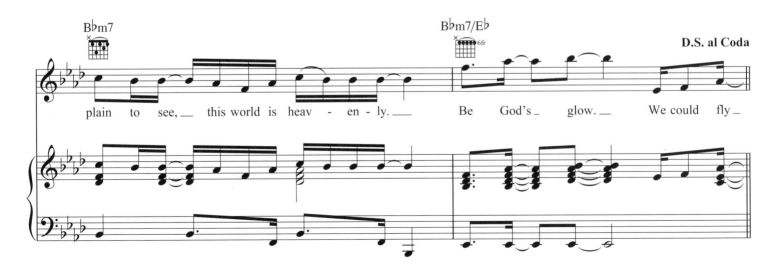

plain to see, __ this world is heav - en - ly. ___ Be God's_ glow. __ We could fly_

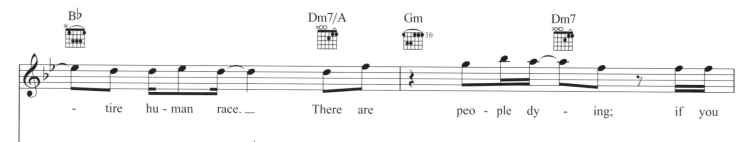

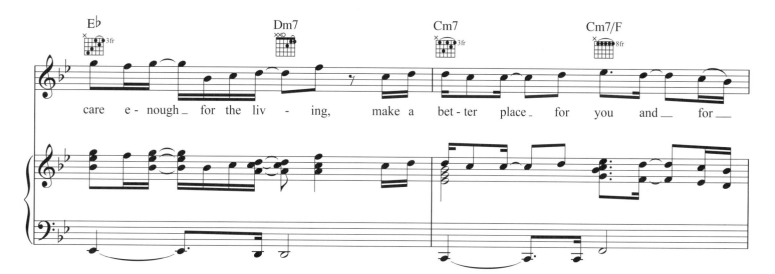

KEEP HOLDING ON

from the Twentieth Century Fox Motion Picture ERAGON

Words and Music by AVRIL LAVIGNE
and LUKASZ GOTTWALD

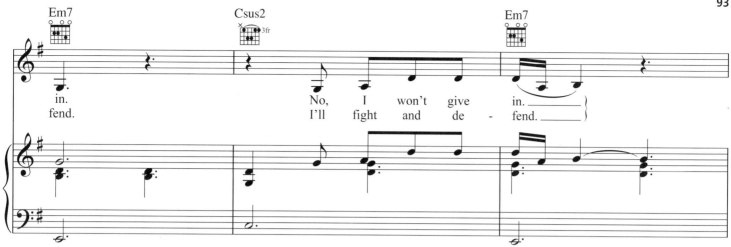

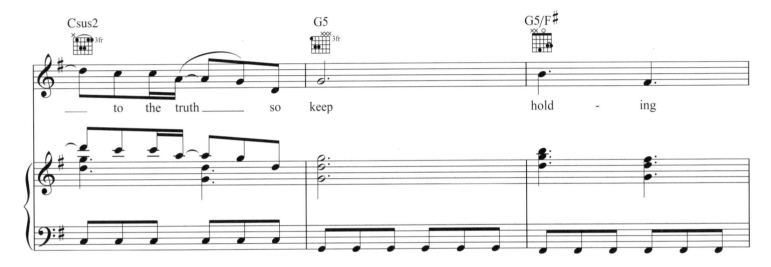

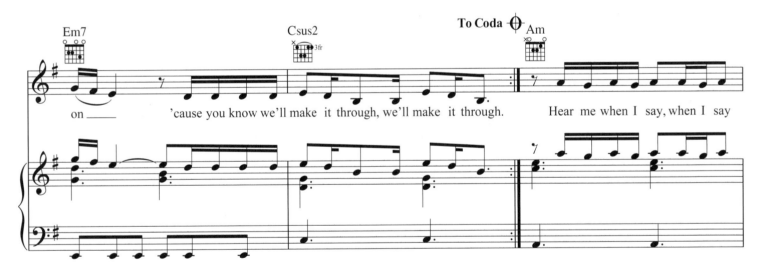

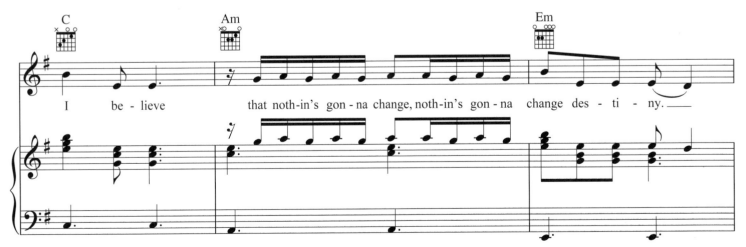

What-ev-er's meant to be will work out per-fect-ly, yeah, _____ yeah,

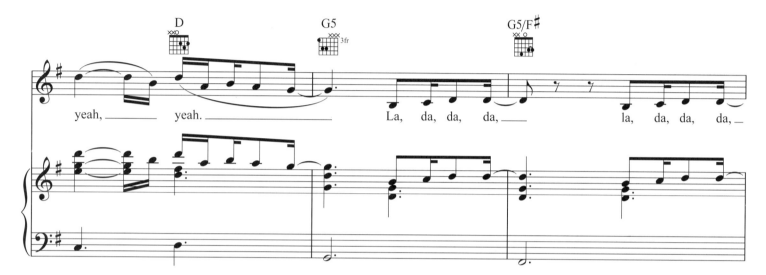

yeah, _____ yeah. _____ La, da, da, da, _____ la, da, da, da, _

la, da, da, da, _____ da, da, _____ da.

D.S. al Coda

CODA

Keep hold - ing on. _____

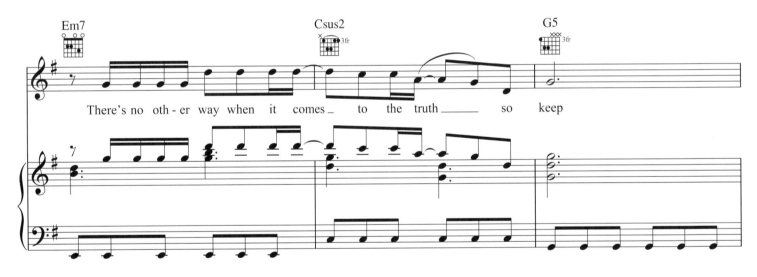

HOME

Words and Music by GREG HOLDEN
and DREW PEARSON

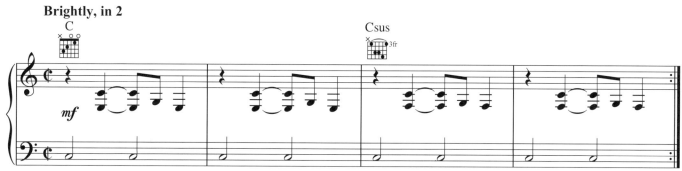

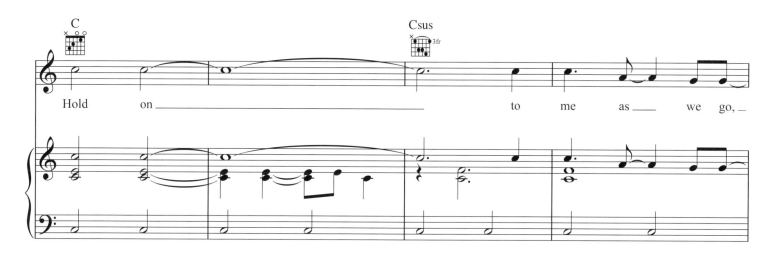

Hold on _____ to me as ___ we go, ___

as we

roll down _____ this

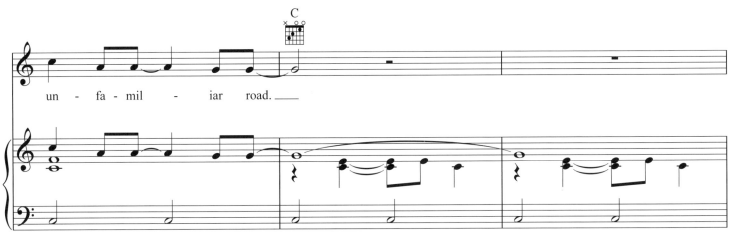

un - fa - mil - iar road. ___

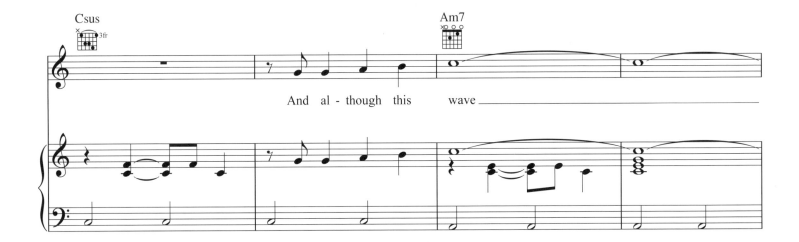

And al - though this wave ___

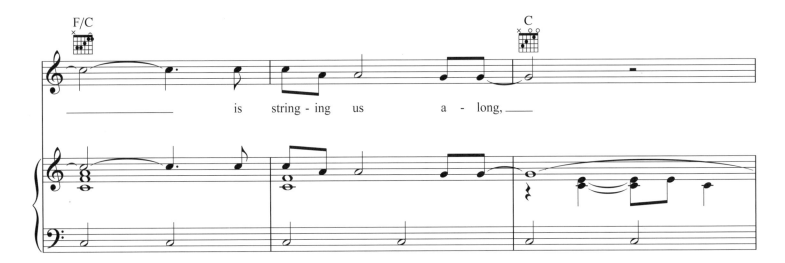

is string - ing us a - long, ___

just know you're

not a - lone, _____ 'cause I'm gon - na

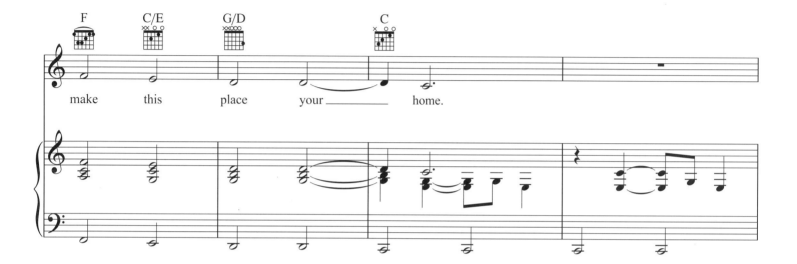

make this place your _____ home.

Set - tle down, _____

it - 'll all be _____ clear.

Don't pay ___ no

mind to ___ the de - mons; ___ they fill you ___ with fear.

Trou - ble, ___ it

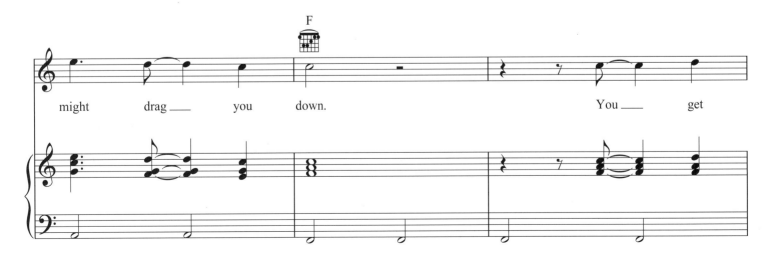

might drag ___ you down. You ___ get

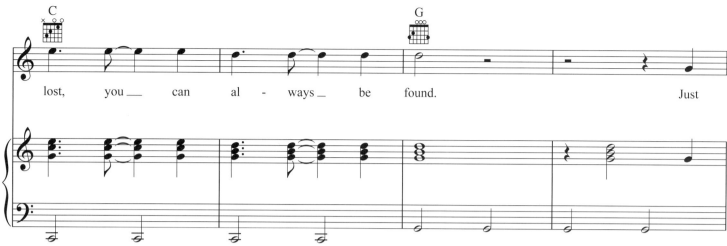

lost, you __ can al - ways __ be found. Just

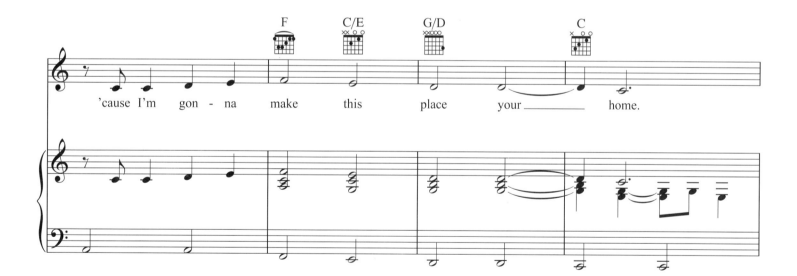

know you're not a - lone, _____

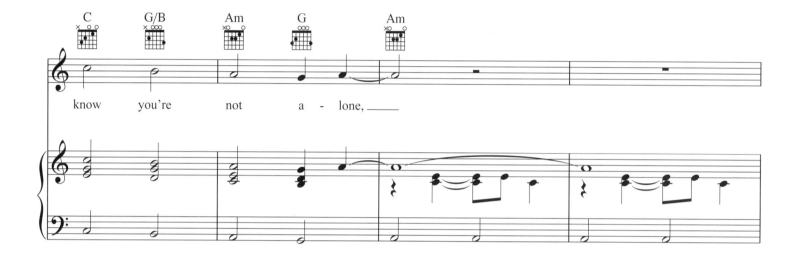

'cause I'm gon - na make this place your _____ home.

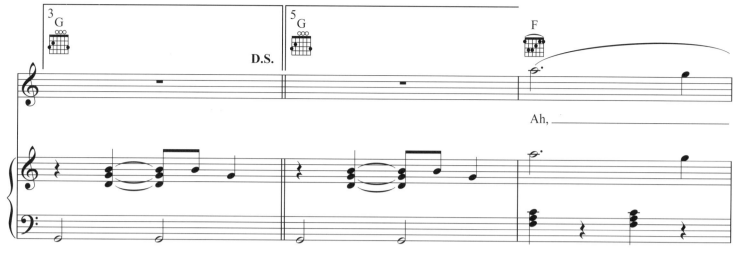

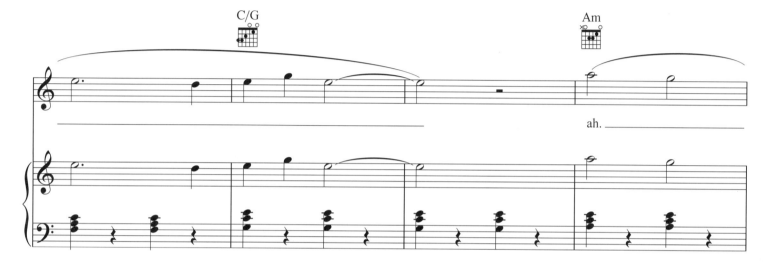

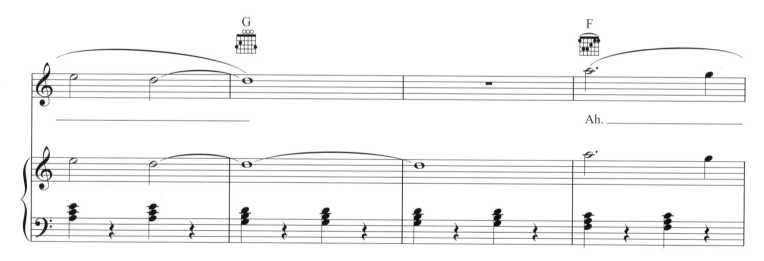

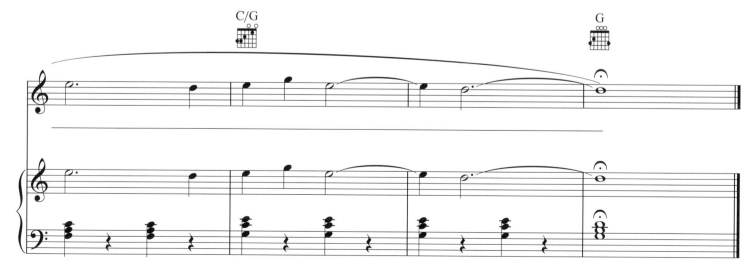

LEAN ON ME

Words and Music by
BILL WITHERS

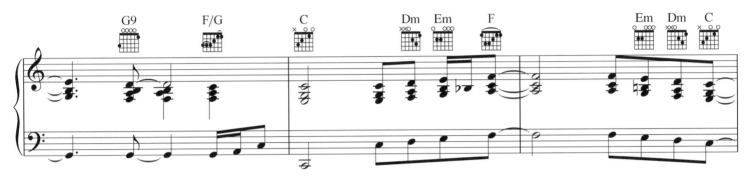

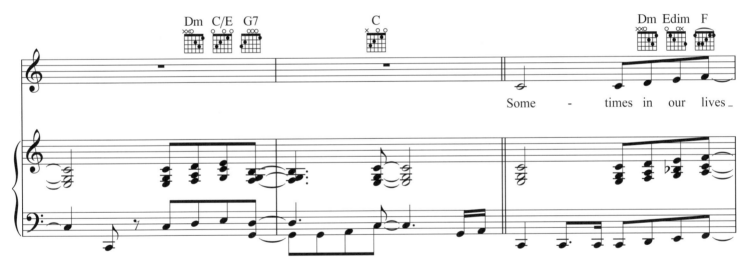

Some - times in our lives_

we all have pain,_ we all have sor - row,_

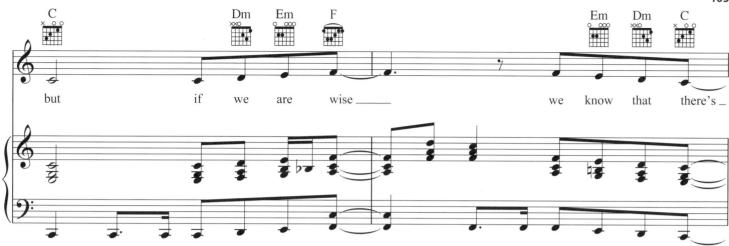

but   if we are wise ____   we know that there's _

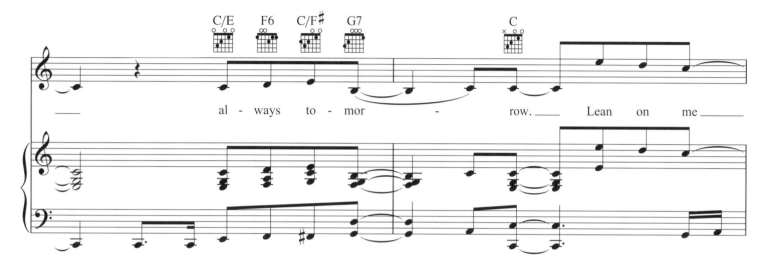

____   al - ways to - mor - row. ____   Lean on me ____

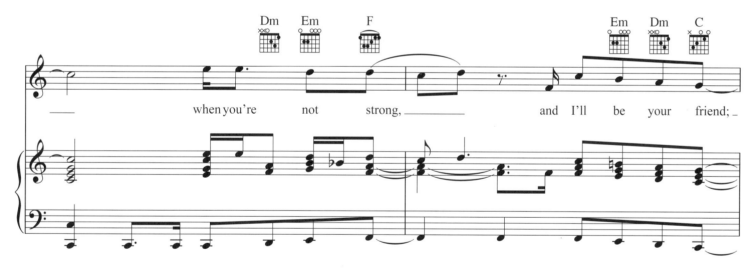

____   when you're not strong, _____   and I'll be your friend; _

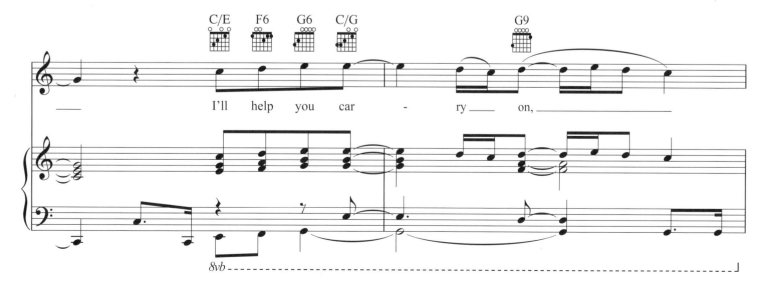

____   I'll help you car - ry ____ on, ____

8vb

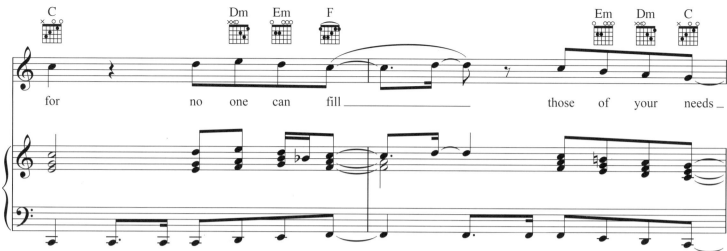

for no one can fill _____ those of your needs _

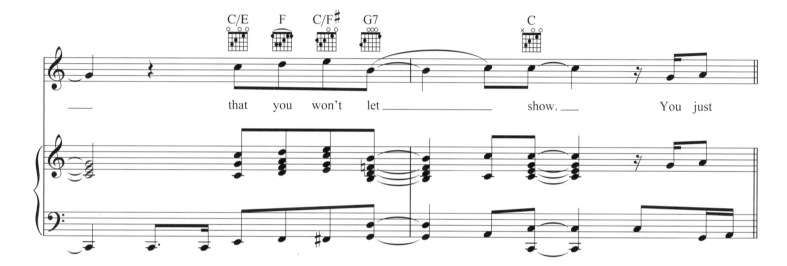

_ that you won't let _____ show. ___ You just

call on me, broth - er, when you need a ____ hand. ___ We all _____

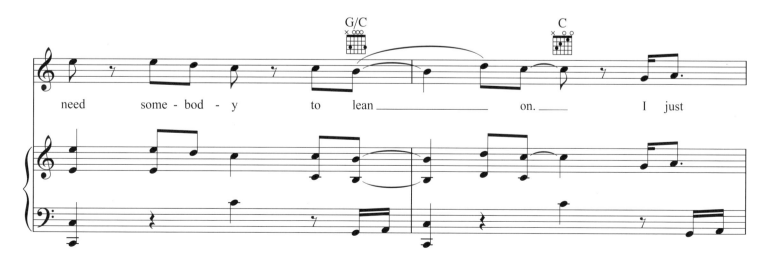

need some - bod - y to lean _____ on. ___ I just

might have a prob-lem that you'll un-der-stand. ___ We all ___

To Coda ⊕

C/E F C/F♯ G7   C

need some-bod-y   to lean ___ on. ___ Lean   on   me

Dm Em   F   Em Dm C

when you're not strong ___   and I'll be your friend; _

C/E F6 G6   G9

___ I'll help you car - ry ___ on, ___

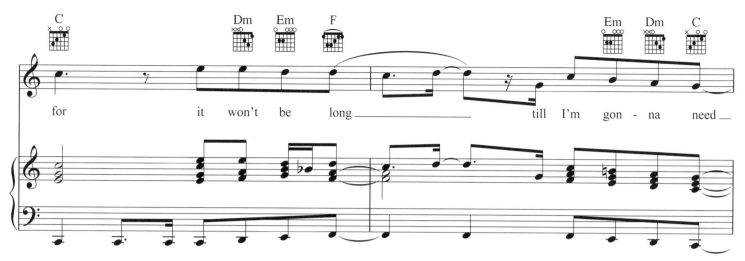

for it won't be long _____ till I'm gon - na need _____

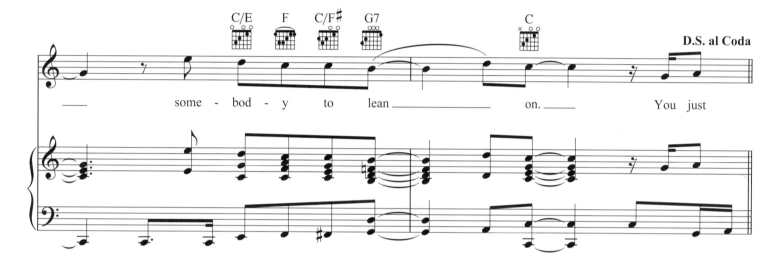

D.S. al Coda

_____ some - bod - y to lean _____ on. _____ You just

CODA

_____ on. _____ If there is a load _____

you have to bear _____ that you can't

8vb -

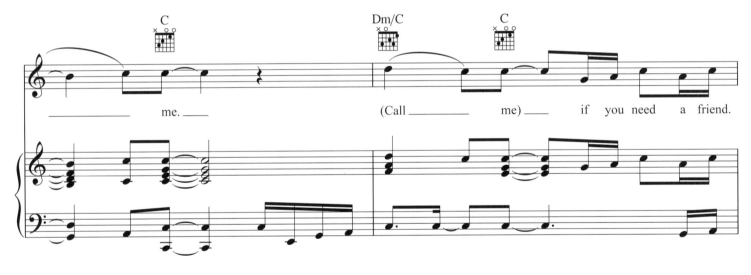

(Call _____ me.) ___ If you ev - er need ___ a friend, call __ me.
(Call _____ me.) ___

(Call _____ me.) ___ Call __ me. ___ (Call _____ me.) ___ Call me.

(Call _____ me.) ___ Call me. ___ (Call _____ me) ___ if you need a friend.

Play 4 times

(Call _____ me.) ___ Call me. Call _____ me. ___

LOVE WINS

Words and Music by DAVID GARCIA,
BRETT JAMES and CARRIE UNDERWOOD

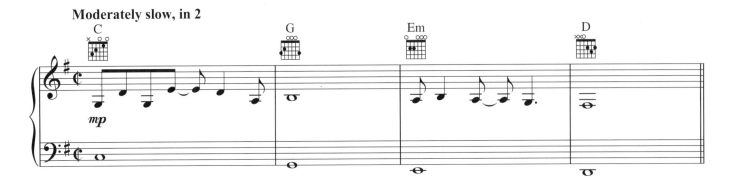

Moderately slow, in 2

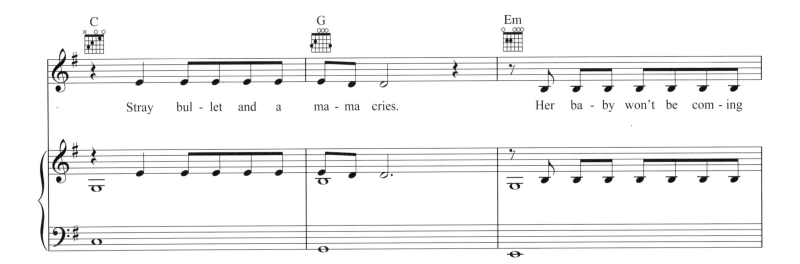

Stray bul-let and a ma-ma cries. Her ba-by won't be com-ing

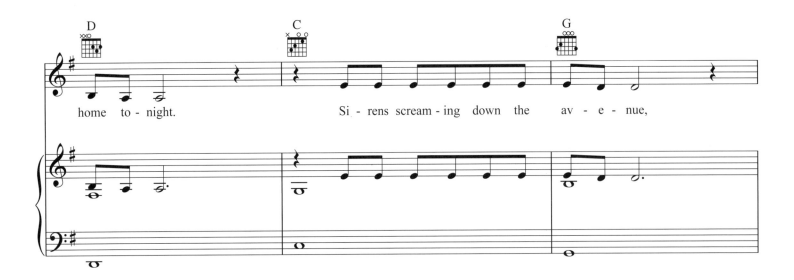

home to-night. Si-rens scream-ing down the av-e-nue,

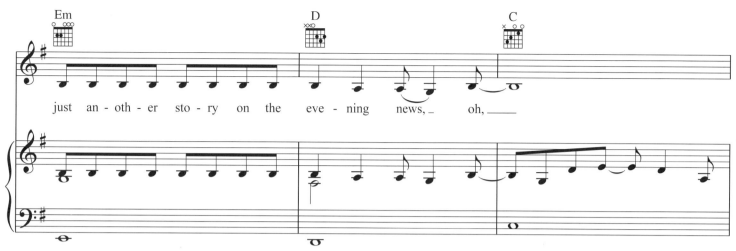

just an-oth-er sto-ry on the eve-ning news,_ oh,_____

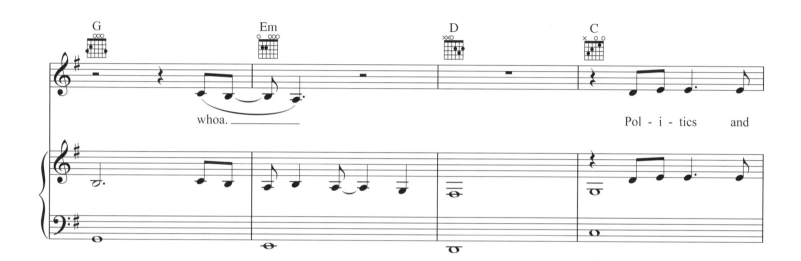

whoa. _____ Pol - i - tics and

prej - u - dice; how the hell'd it ev - er come to this?

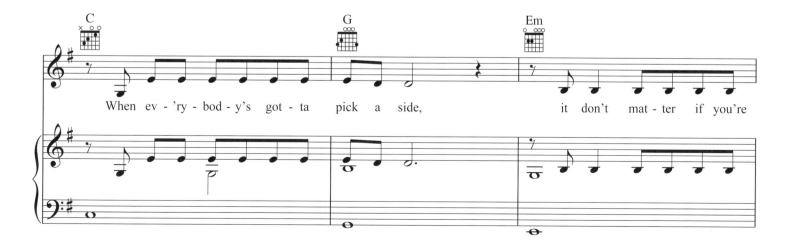

When ev - 'ry-bod-y's got - ta pick a side, it don't mat - ter if you're

wrong or right, __ no. _____ And so it goes, _____ but I hold __

__ on to hope __ and I won't __ let go, __ 'cause __ I, _____

__ I __ be - lieve __ you __ and me are sis - ters and broth - ers. And

I, _____ I __ be - lieve we're made __ to be

here for each oth - er. And we'll nev - er fall if we walk hand in hand, put a

world that seems bro - ken to - geth - er a - gain. Yeah, I,_____

I____ be - lieve   in____ the end,   love

To Coda ⊕

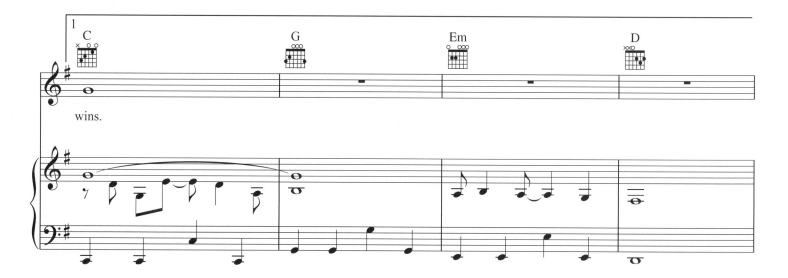

wins.

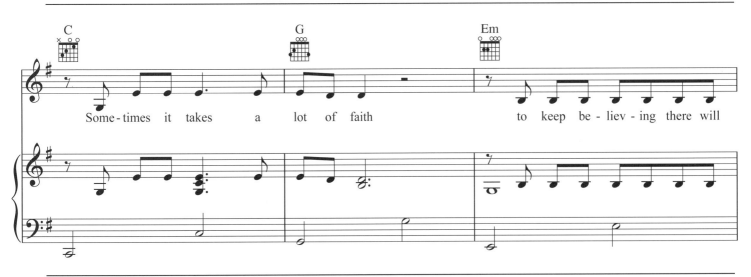

Some-times it takes a lot of faith to keep be-liev-ing there will

come a day when the tears and the sad-ness, the pain and the hate, the

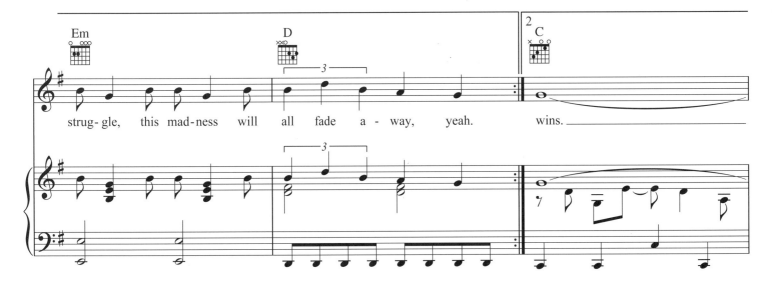

strug-gle, this mad-ness will all fade a-way, yeah. wins.

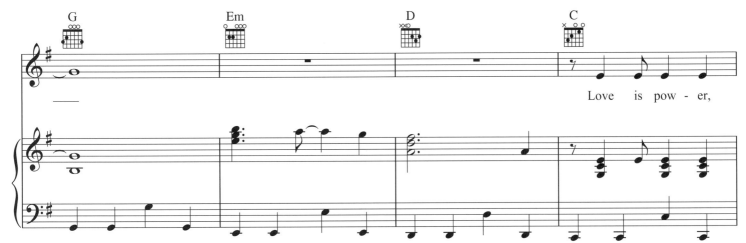

Love is pow-er,

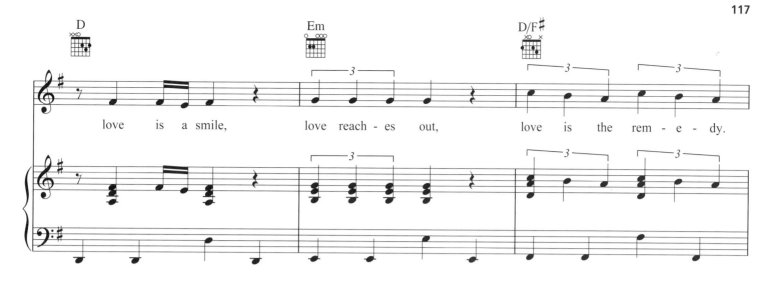

love is a smile, love reach - es out, love is the rem - e - dy.

Love is the an - swer, love's an o - pen door, love is the on - ly thing

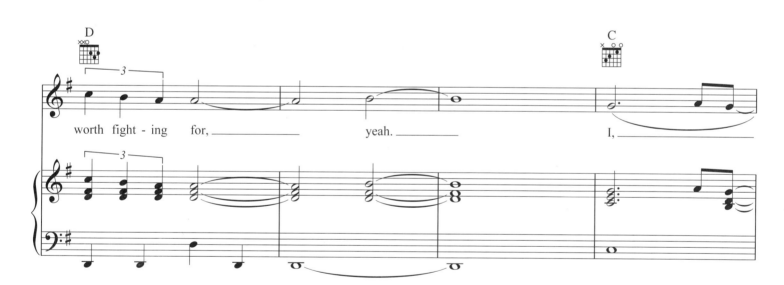

worth fight - ing for, _____ yeah. _____ I, _____

D.S. al Coda

N.C.

_____ I ___ be - lieve you ___ and me are sis - ters and broth - ers. And

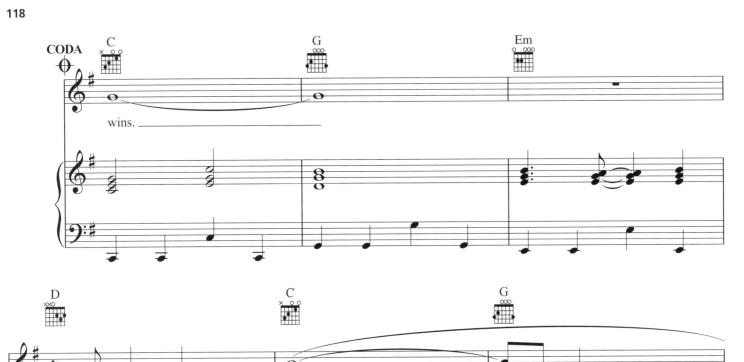

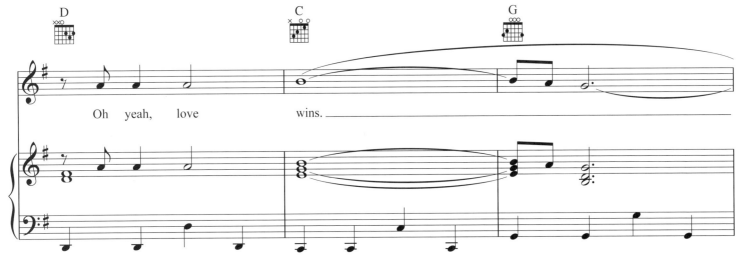

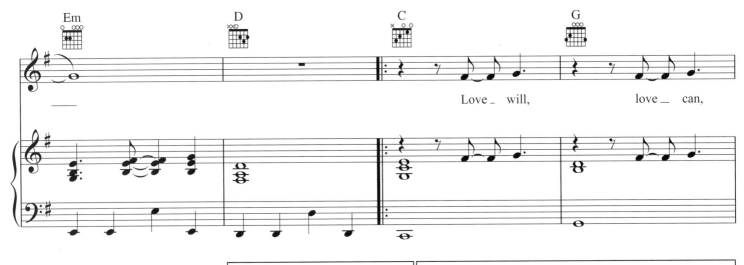

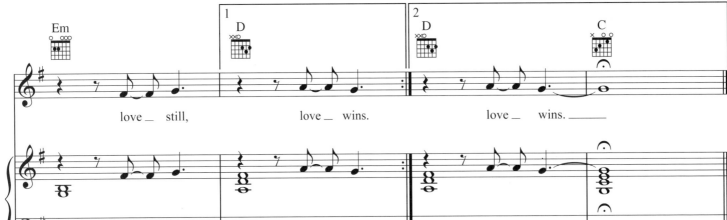

I'M A RISER

Words and Music by TRAVIS MEADOWS
and STEVEN MOAKLER

Moderate Country Rock

Lay your pret-ty head___ down on___ my shoul - der;

you don't have to wor - ry an - y - more.___

This old world is cold __ and get - ting cold __ - er, and

I know how to lock __ and bolt the door. __ I'm

strong e - nough to hold __ you through the win - ter, and I
we ain't got __ no mon - ey, I can make __ it,

mean e - nough __ to stare __ your de - mons __ down. The hard
ain't a - fraid __ of work - ing to the __ bone. When I don't __

times put the shine in-to the dia - mond.
know what I'm do - ing, I can fake it. I'll

I won't let that keep us in the ground.
pray 'til Je - sus rolls a - way the stone. I'm a

ris - er, I'm a "get up off the ground, don't run and hid - er."

Push-ing comes to shove and, hey, I'm a fight - er. When

dark - ness comes to town, __ I'm a light - er,

a "get out __ a - liv - er" of the fi - re, sur - viv -

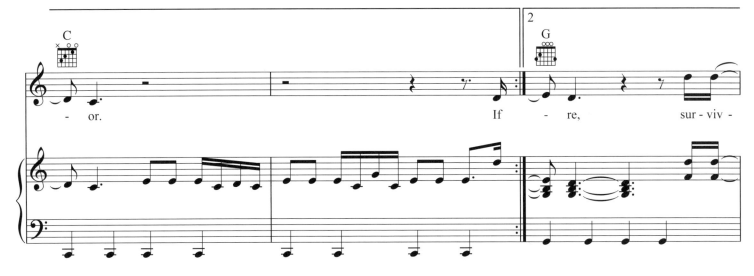

- or. If - re, sur - viv -

- or. _____

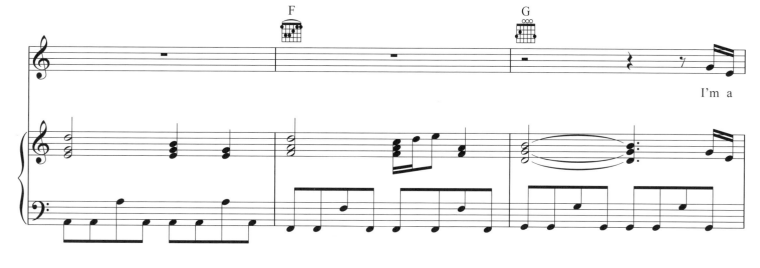

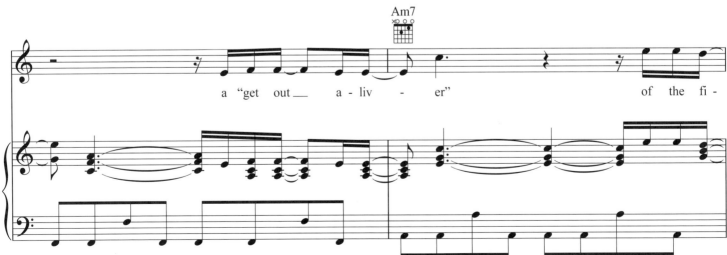

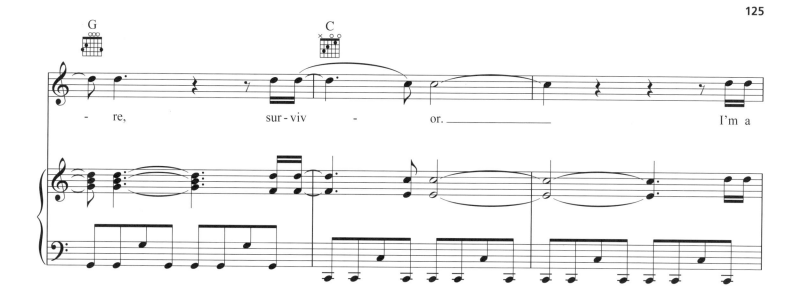

-re, sur - viv - or._____ I'm a

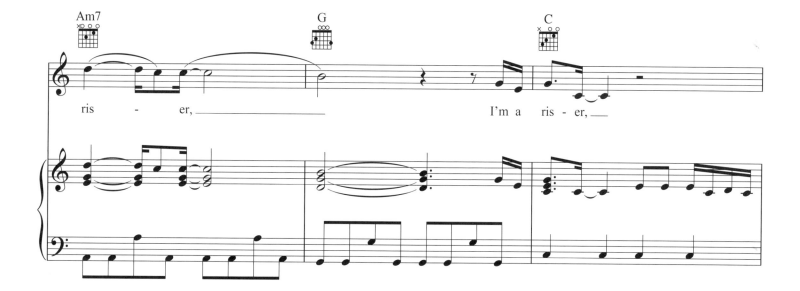

ris - er,_____ I'm a ris - er,___

I'm a ris - er.

ONE CALL AWAY

Words and Music by CHARLIE PUTH,
JUSTIN FRANKS, BREYAN ISAAC,
MATT PRIME, BLAKE ANTHONY CARTER
and MAUREEN McDONALD

With a soulful beat

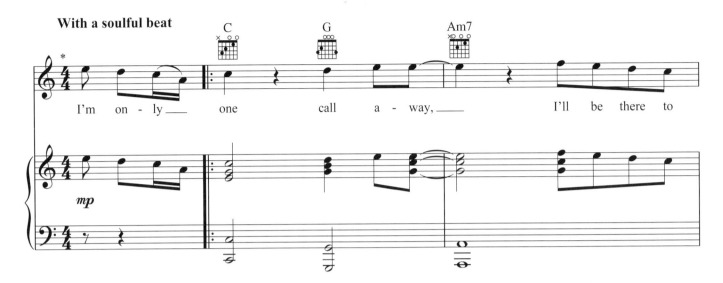

* *Recorded a half step higher.*

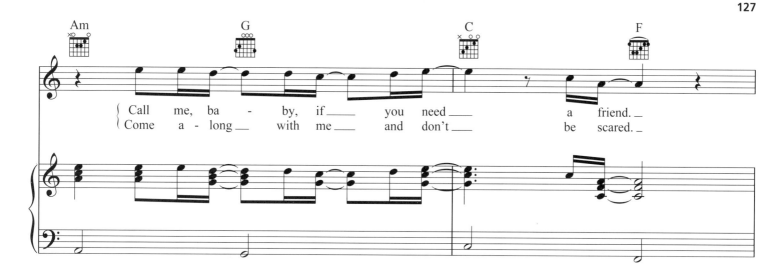

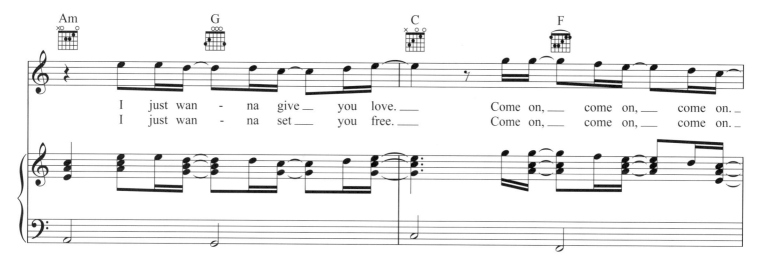

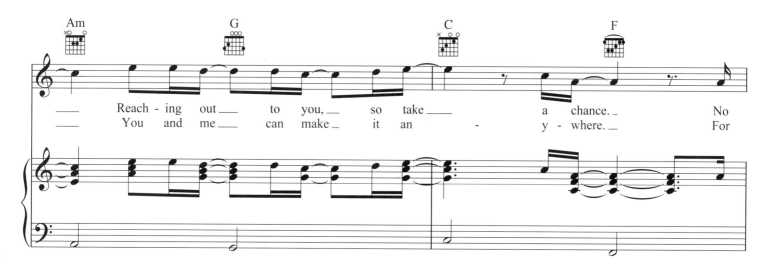

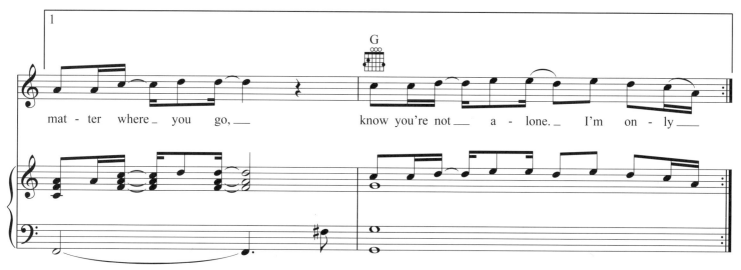

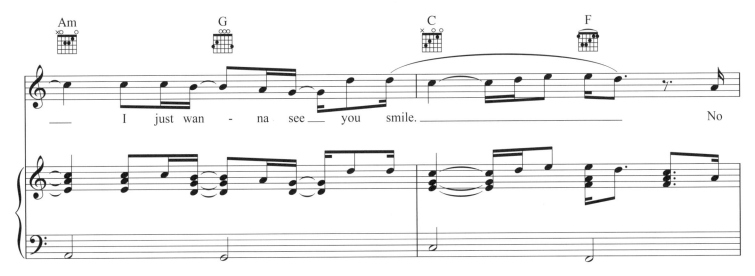

save the _____ day. _____ Su - per - man _____ got _____ noth - ing on me, _____

_____ I'm on - ly ____ one call a - way. ____ And when you're

weak, I'll be strong. ____ I'm gon - na keep hold - ing on. _____

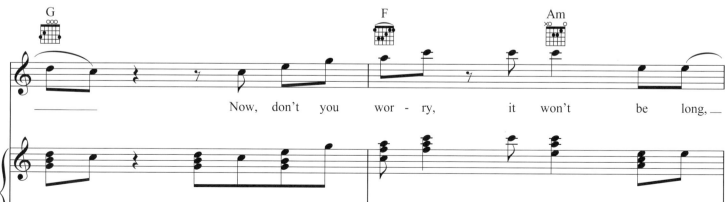

Now, don't you wor - ry, it won't be long, _____

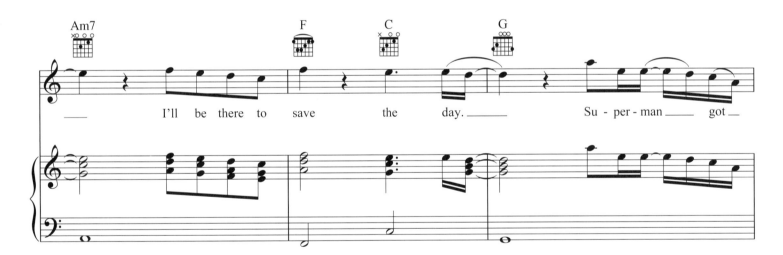

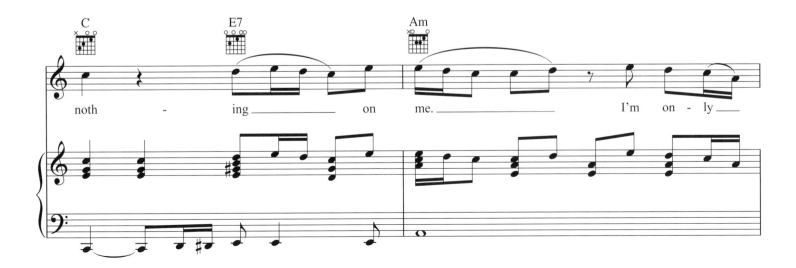

OOH CHILD

Words and Music by
STAN VINCENT

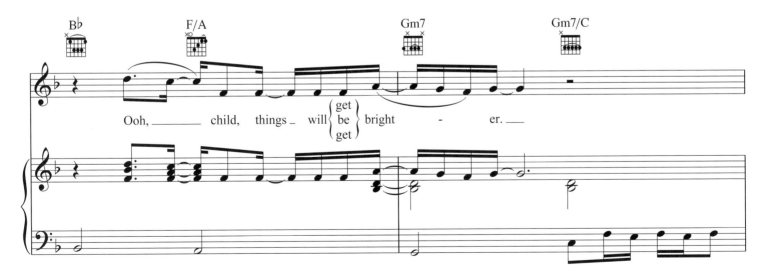

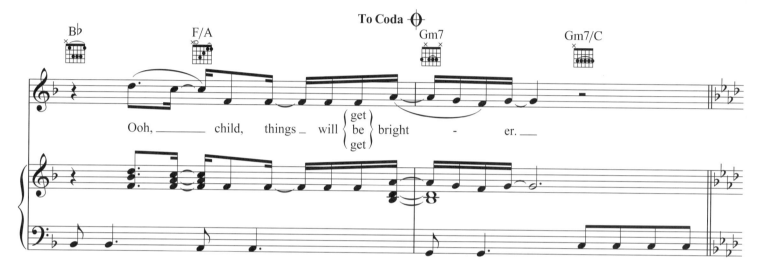

Some - day, yeah, __ we'll walk in the rays of a beau-ti-ful sun; __

some - day, when the world is much bright - er. __

La - la - la - la - la - la - la - la - la - la - la. __

La - la - la - la - la - la - la - la - la. __

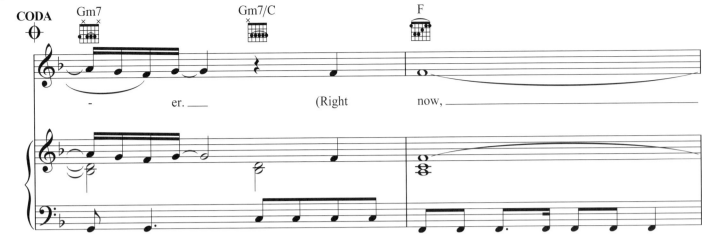

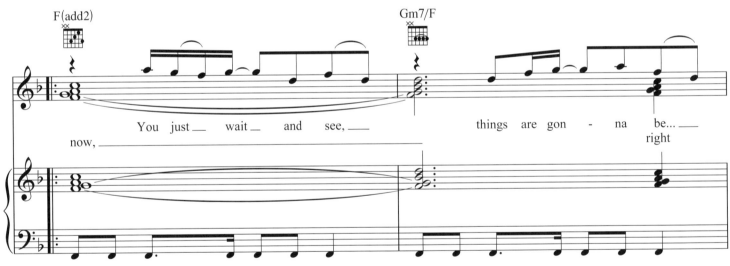

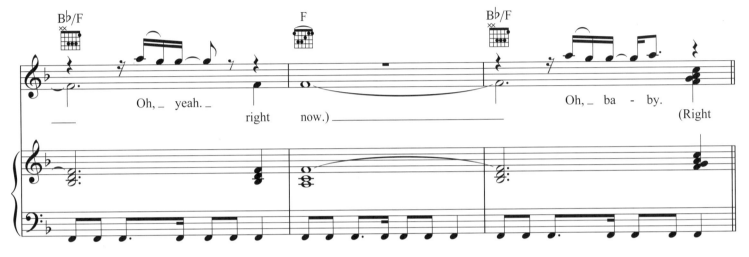

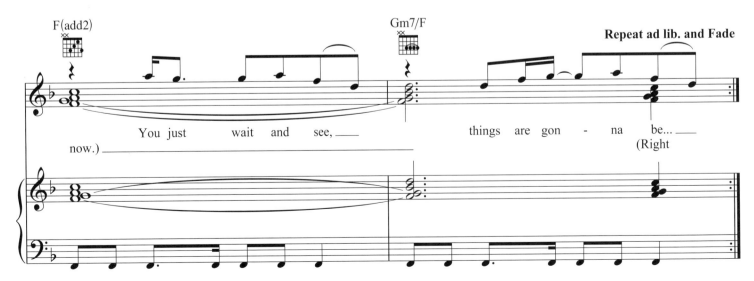

ONE LOVE

Words and Music by
BOB MARLEY

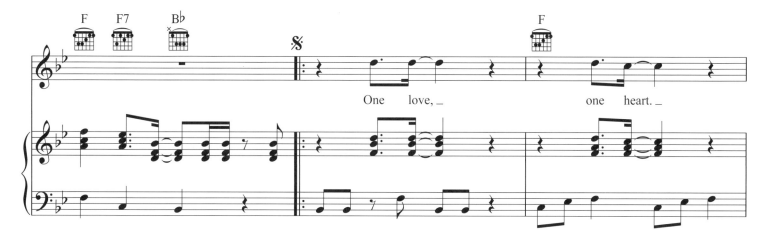

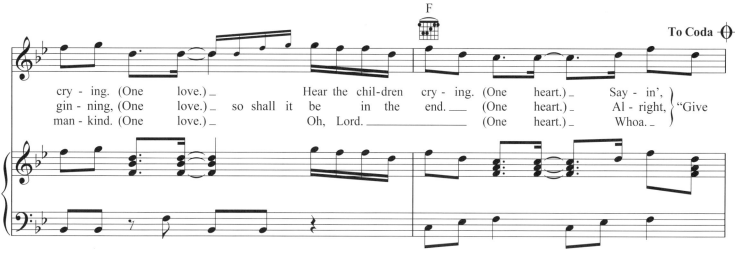

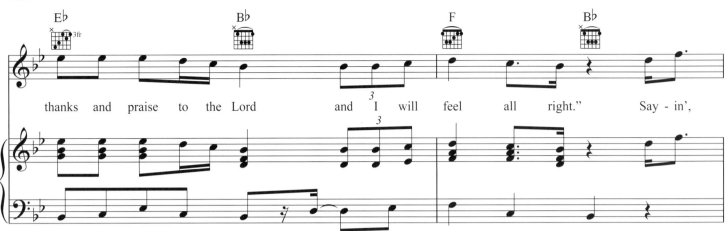

thanks and praise to the Lord and I will feel all right." Say - in',

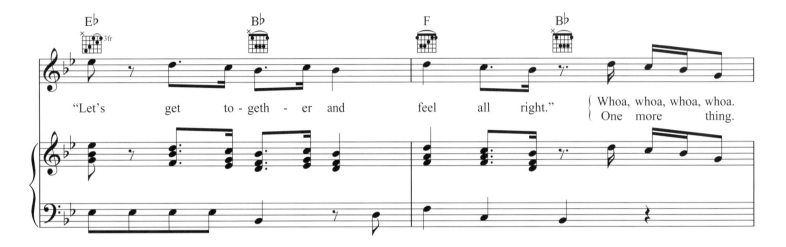

"Let's get to - geth - er and feel all right." Whoa, whoa, whoa, whoa. / One more thing.

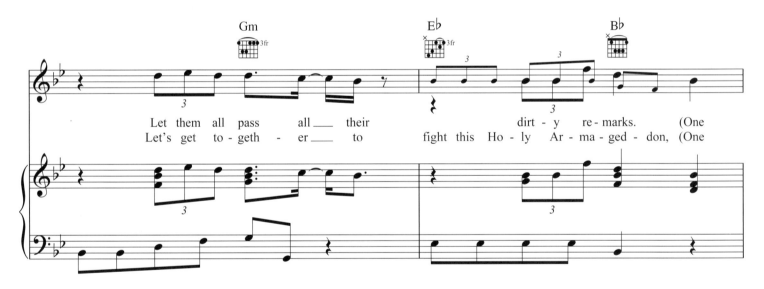

Let them all pass all ___ their dirt - y re - marks. (One
Let's get to - geth - er ___ to fight this Ho - ly Ar - ma - ged - don, (One

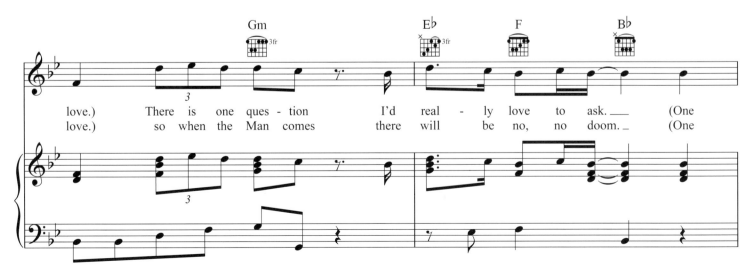

love.) There is one ques - tion I'd real - ly love to ask. ___ (One
love.) so when the Man comes there will be no, no doom. _ (One

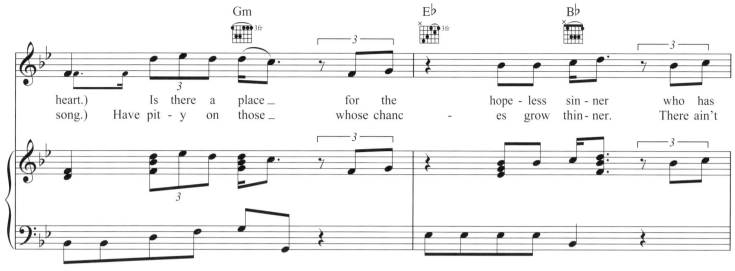

heart.)   Is there a place ___   for the   hope - less sin - ner   who has
song.)   Have pit - y on those ___   whose chanc - es   grow thin - ner.   There ain't

hurt all man - kind   just to   save his own? ___ Be - lieve me.
no hid - ing place   from the

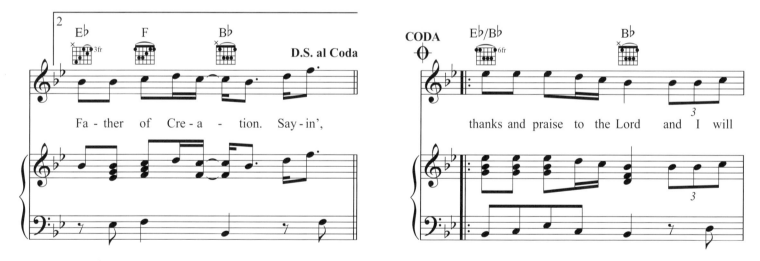

Fa - ther of Cre - a - tion. Say - in',

CODA

thanks and praise to the Lord   and I will

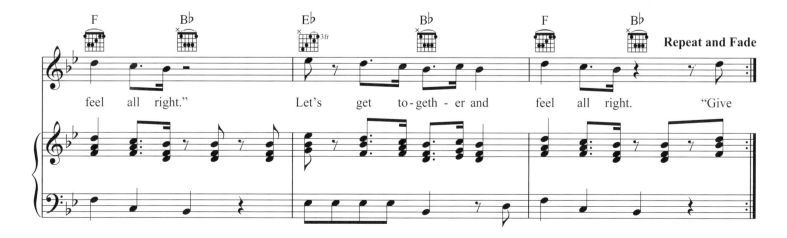

feel all right."   Let's get to - geth - er and   feel all right.   "Give

RISE

Words and Music by KATY PERRY,
ALI PAYAMI, MAX MARTIN
and SAVAN KOTECHA

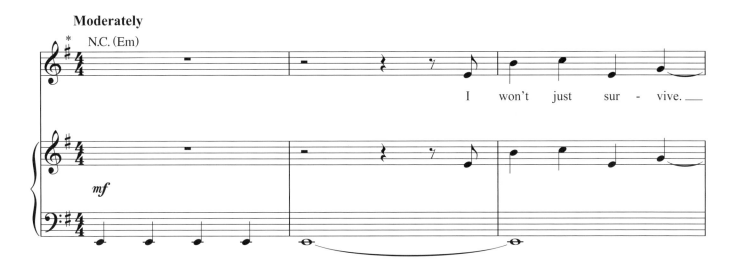

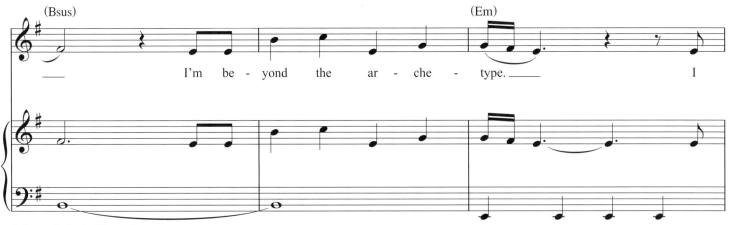

* *Recorded a half step lower.*

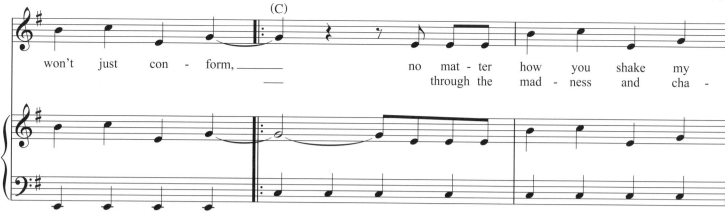

won't just con - form, _____ no mat - ter how you shake my
_____ through the mad - ness and my cha -

core. _____ 'Cause my roots, they run deep, _____ oh. _____
os, _____ so I call on my an - gels. _____ They say, _

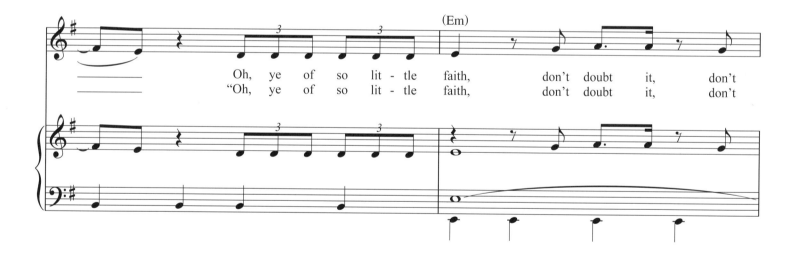

Oh, ye of so lit - tle faith, don't doubt it, don't
"Oh, ye of so lit - tle faith, don't doubt it, don't

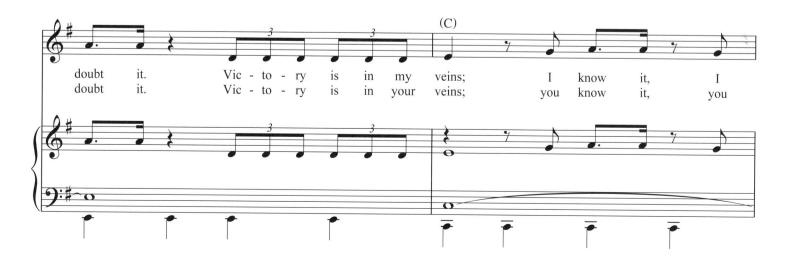

doubt it. Vic - to - ry is in my veins; I know it, I
doubt it. Vic - to - ry is in your veins; you know it, you

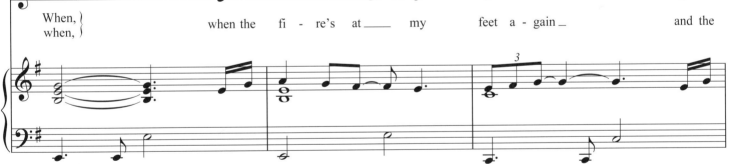

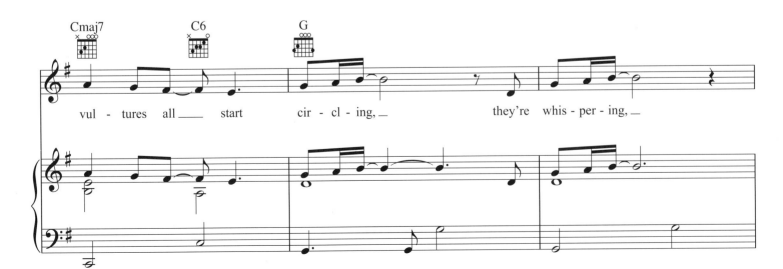

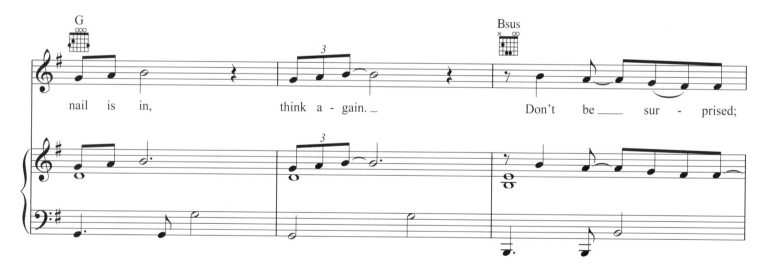

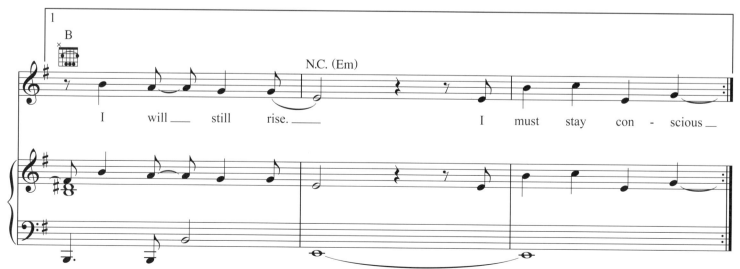

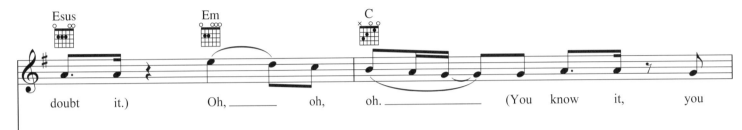

STAND BY ME

Words and Music by JERRY LEIBER,
MIKE STOLLER and BEN E. KING

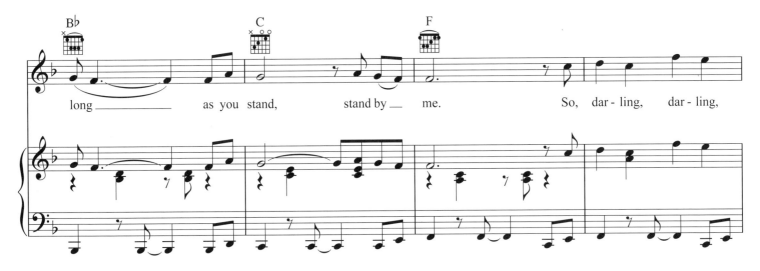

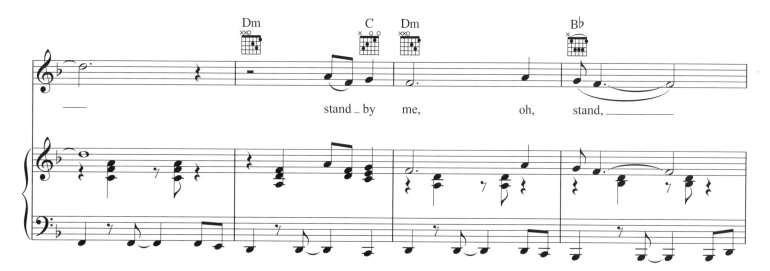

RISE UP

Words and Music by CASSANDRA BATIE
and JENNIFER DECILVEO

Recorded a half step higher.

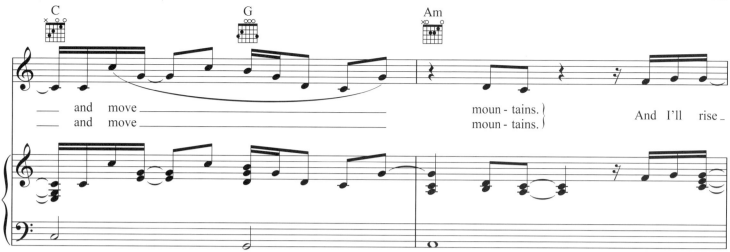

_____ and move _____ moun - tains.)
_____ and move _____ moun - tains.)   And I'll rise _

_____ up, I'll rise _____ like the day. _ I'll rise _____ up, I'll rise _____ un - a - fraid. I'll rise _

To Coda ⊕

_____ up   and I'll do it a thou - sand _____ times a - gain.   And I'll rise _

_____ up   high _ like the waves. _ I'll rise _____ up   in spite _ of the ache. _ I'll rise _

up and I'll do it a thou - sand _____ times a - gain _____ for you, _

for you, _____

you, _____ for you. _____

D.C. al Coda

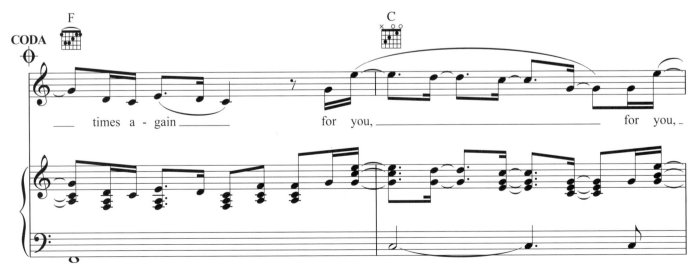

CODA

_ times a - gain _____ for you, _____ for you, _

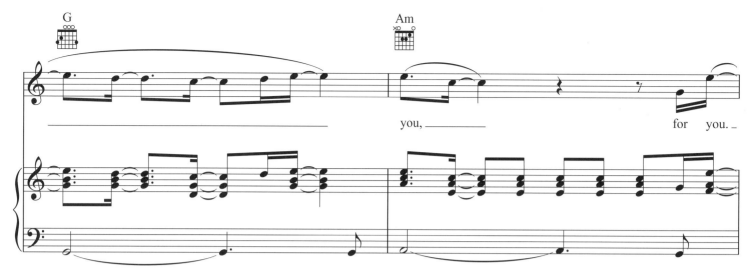

you, _____ for you. _

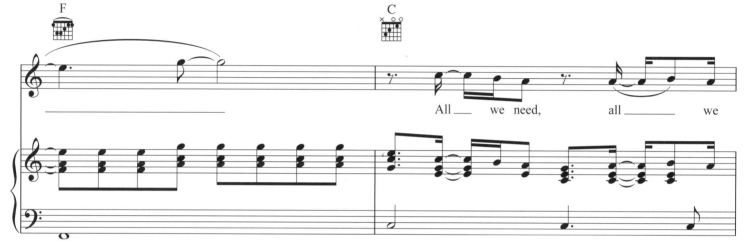

All ___ we need, all _____ we

need is _____ hope. _ And for that we have each ___ oth - er, _____ and for that we have each _

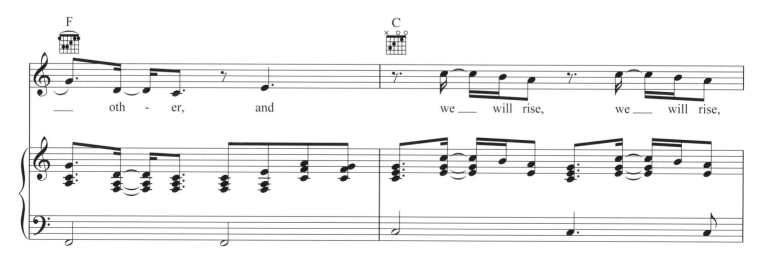

___ oth - er, _____ and we ___ will rise, we ___ will rise,

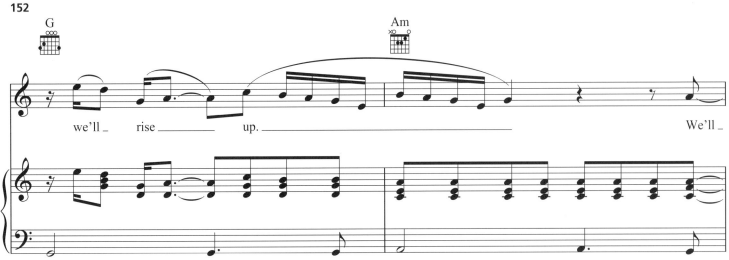

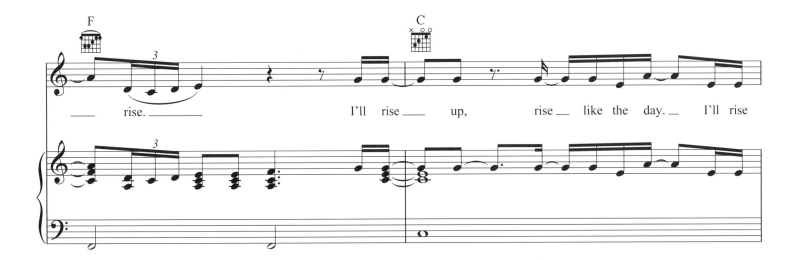

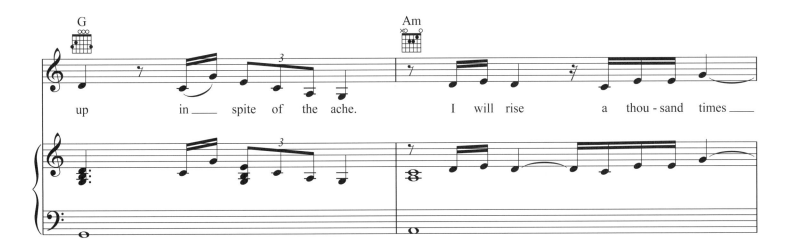

up in spite_ of the ache._ We'll rise_ up and we'll do it a thou-sand_

times a-gain _____ for you, _____ for you, _____

you, _____ for you. _____ (Hm, hm, _____

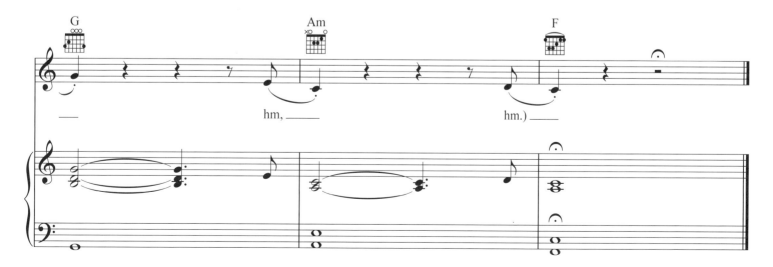

_____ hm, _____ hm.) _____

STAND BY YOU

Words and Music by RACHEL PLATTEN,
JOY WILLIAMS, JACK ANTONOFF,
JON LEVINE and MATTHEW B. MORRIS

E - ven if we can't find heav- en, heav- en,

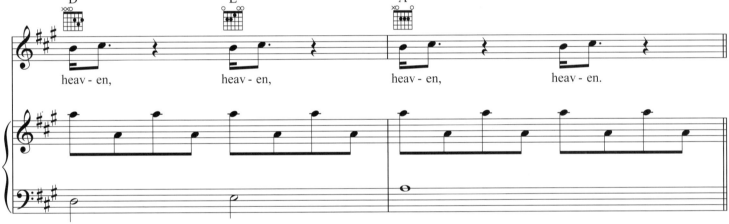

heav - en, heav - en, heav - en, heav - en.

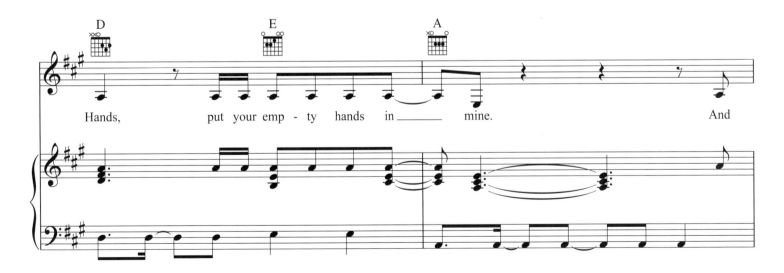

Hands, put your emp - ty hands in _____ mine. And

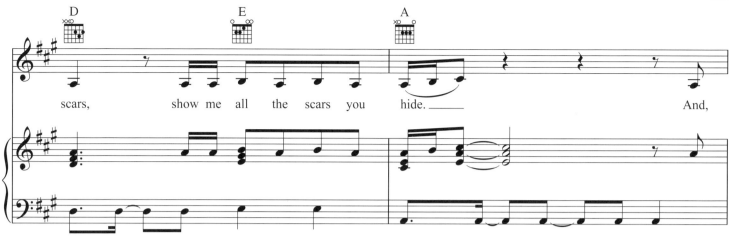

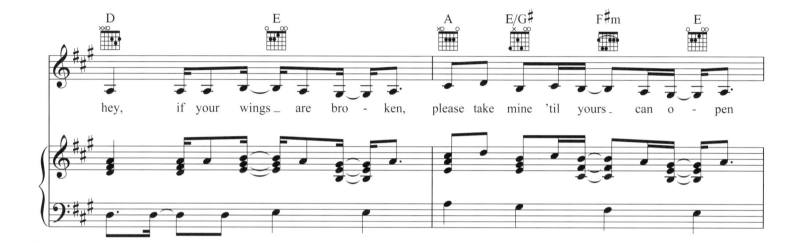

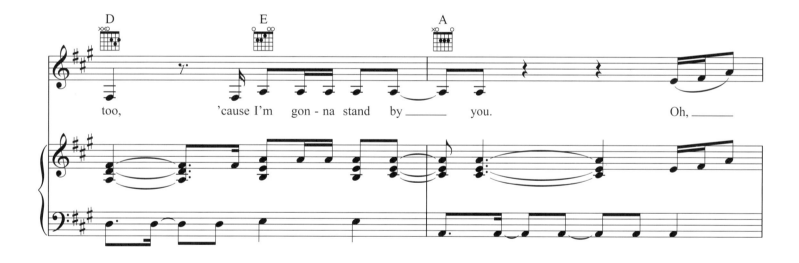

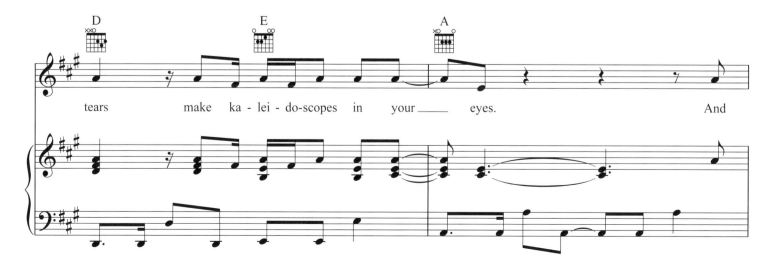

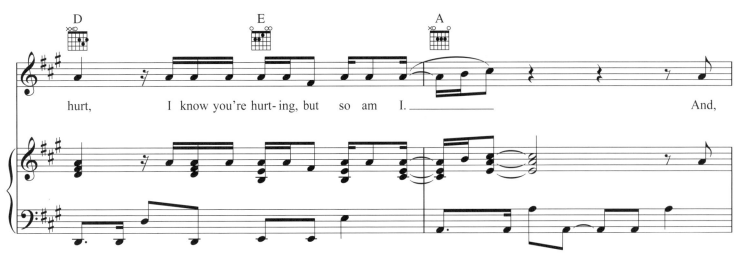

hurt, I know you're hurt-ing, but so am I. _____ And,

love, _ if your wings _ are bro - ken, bor-row mine _ so yours _ can o - pen too, _

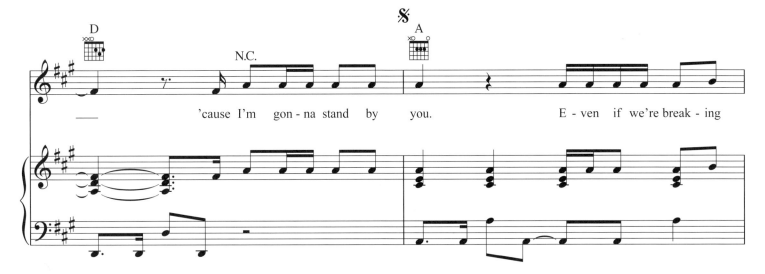

_ 'cause I'm gon - na stand by you. E - ven if we're break - ing

down, _ we can find a way to break through. _ E - ven if we can't find

heav-en, I'll walk through hell with you. Love, _____ you're not a-lone, _____

_____ 'cause I'm gon-na stand by you. E-ven if we can't find

heav-en, I'm gon-na stand by you. _____ E-ven if we can't find

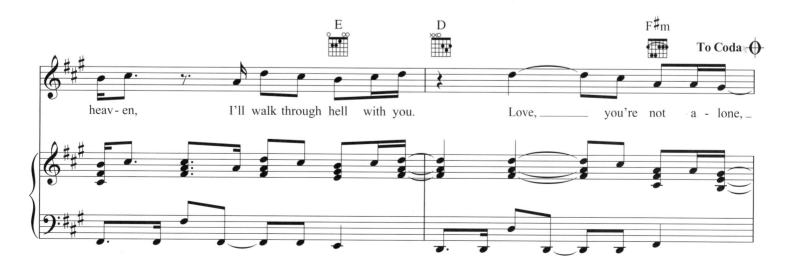

heav-en, I'll walk through hell with you. Love, _____ you're not a-lone, _____

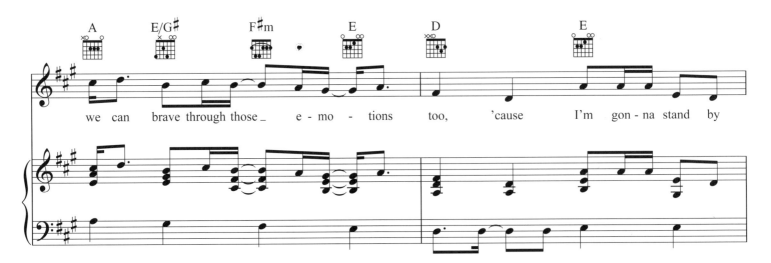

you. And, oh, _____ truth, I guess truth is what _ you be-

lieve in. And faith, I think faith is hav - ing a

rea - son. _ And I know, _ know, love, if your wings _ are bro - ken,

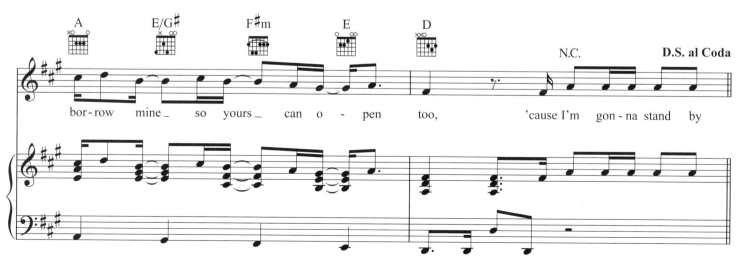

bor - row mine _ so yours _ can o - pen too, 'cause I'm gon-na stand by

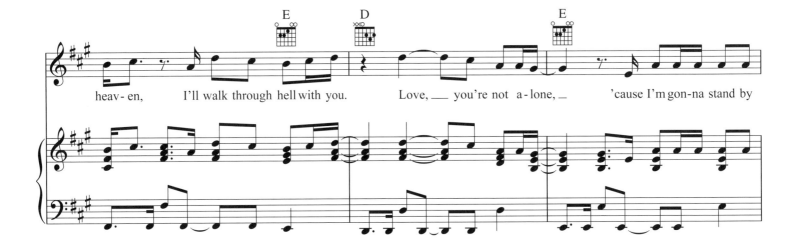

SUPERHEROES

Words and Music by DANNY O'DONOGHUE,
MARK SHEEHAN and JAMES BARRY

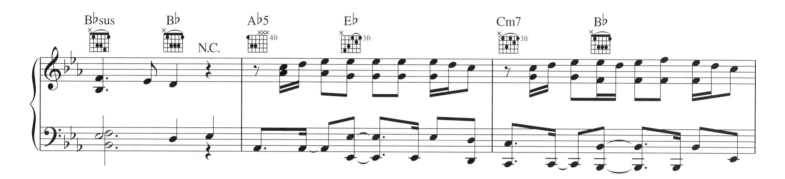

All her life, ___ she has seen ___ all the mean-

-er side ___ of mean. ___ They took a-way ___ the proph-et's dream ___ for a prof-

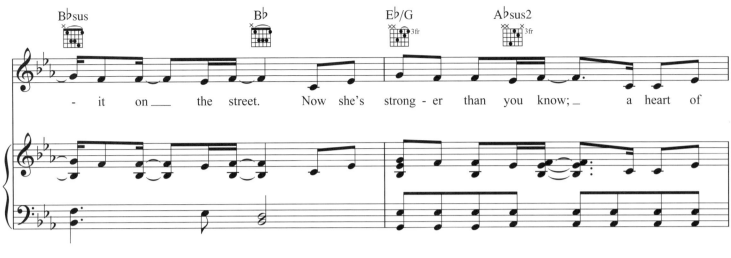

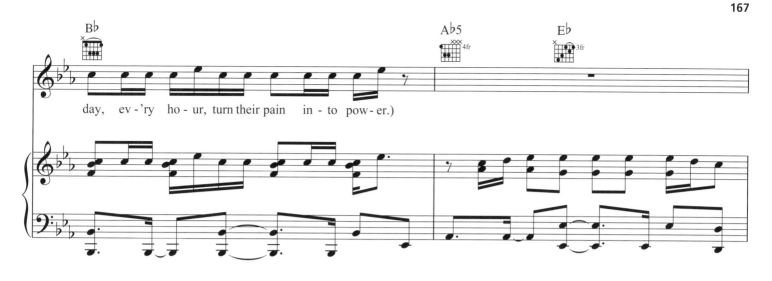

day, ev-'ry ho-ur, turn their pain in-to pow-er.)

(Ev-'ry

She's got li-ons in her heart, a fi-re in her soul. He's got a
day, ev-'ry ho-ur, turn their pain in-to pow-er.)

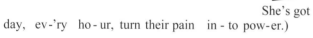

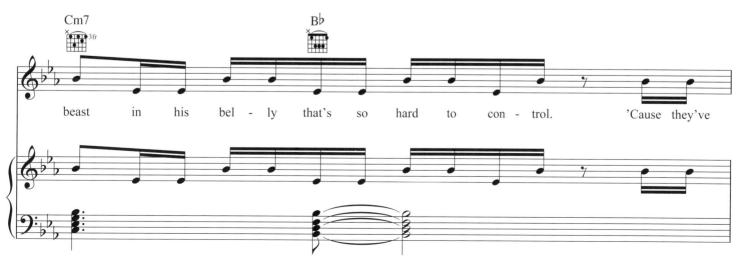

beast in his bel-ly that's so hard to con-trol. 'Cause they've

D.S. al Coda
(take 2nd ending)

ex - plode, ex - plode, ex - plode. When you've been fight - ing for it

CODA

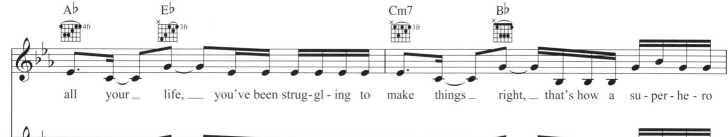

day, ev - 'ry ho - ur, turn their pain in - to pow - er.)

When you've been fight - ing for it

all your life, you've been strug - gl - ing to make things right, that's how a su - per - he - ro

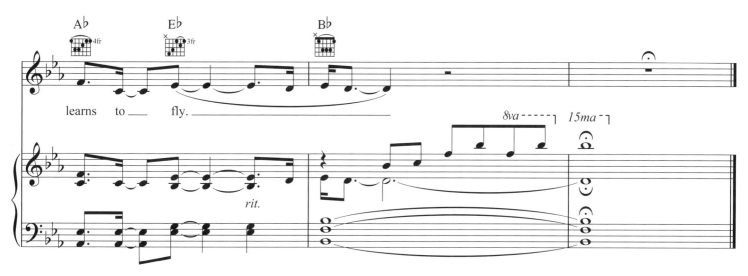

learns to fly.

TOMORROW
from the Musical Production ANNIE

Lyric by MARTIN CHARNIN
Music by CHARLES STROUSE

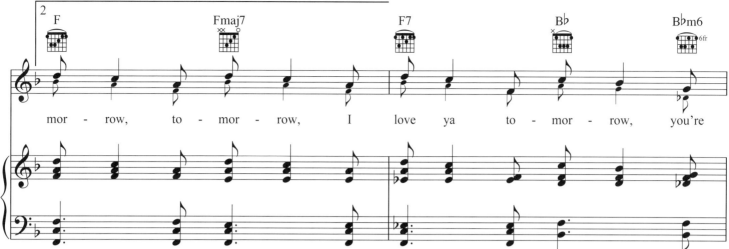

mor - row, to - mor - row, I love ya to - mor - row, you're

{ al - ways } { on - ly } a day a - way! To - mor - row, to - mor - row, I

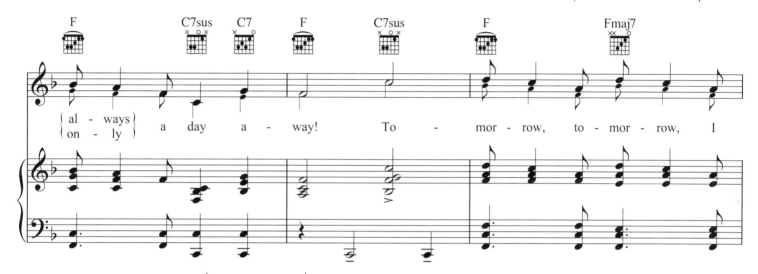

love ya to - mor - row, you're { al - ways } { on - ly } a day a -

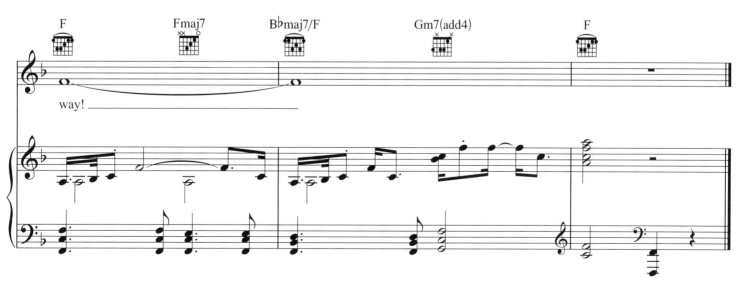

way! _____

UNDERDOG

Words and Music by ALICIA AUGELLO-COOK,
ED SHEERAN, AMY WADGE,
FOY VANCE, JONNY COFFER
and JOHNNY McDAID

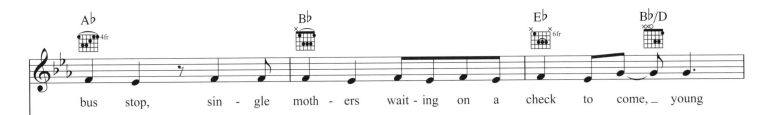

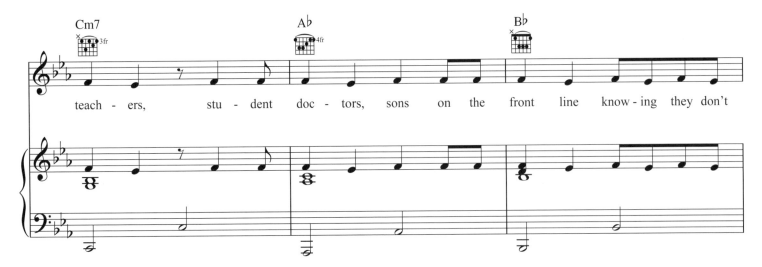

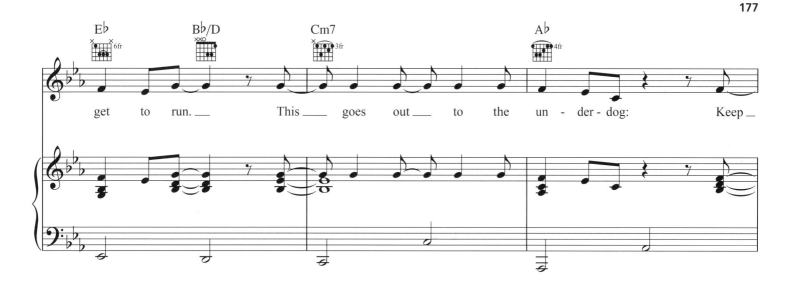

get to run. __ This __ goes out __ to the un - der - dog: Keep __

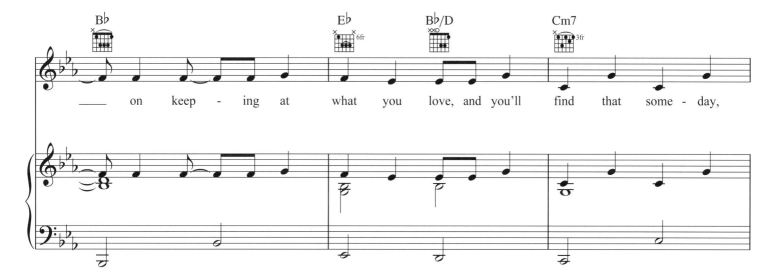

__ on keep - ing at what you love, and you'll find that some - day,

soon e - nough, you will rise up, rise __ up, yeah. __

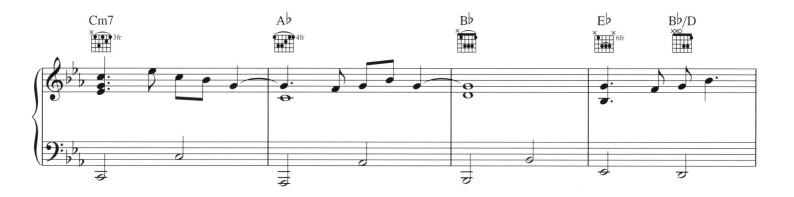

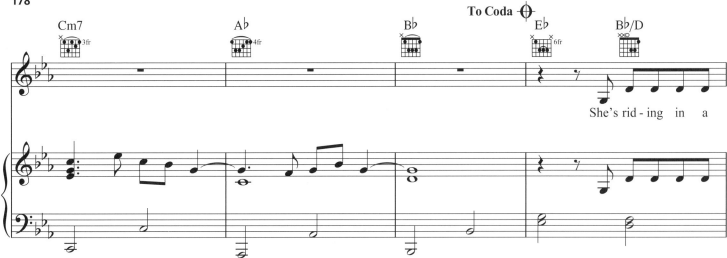

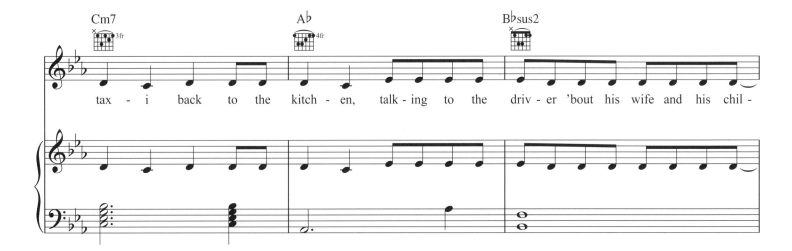

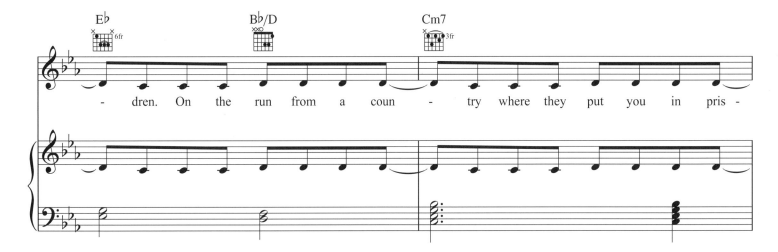

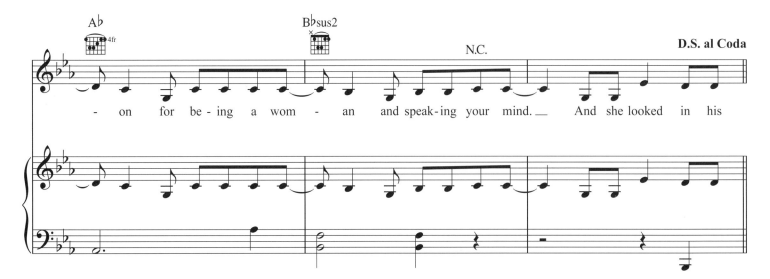

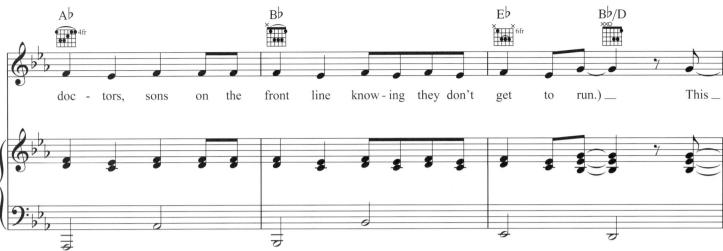

doc - tors, sons on the front line know - ing they don't get to run.) __ This __

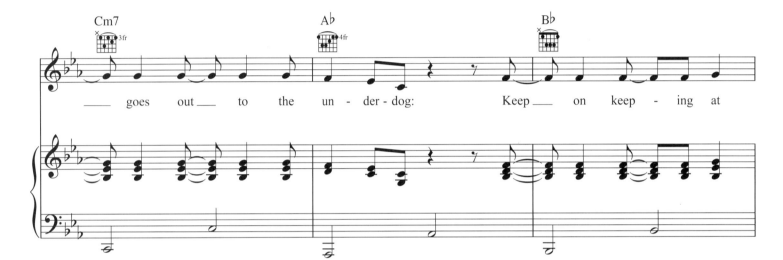

__ goes out __ to the un - der - dog: Keep __ on keep - ing at

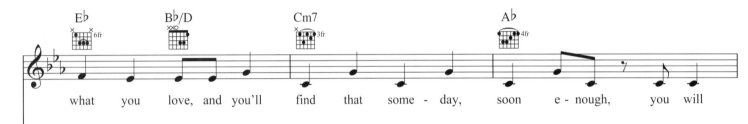

what you love, and you'll find that some - day, soon e - nough, you will

rise up, rise __ up, yeah. __

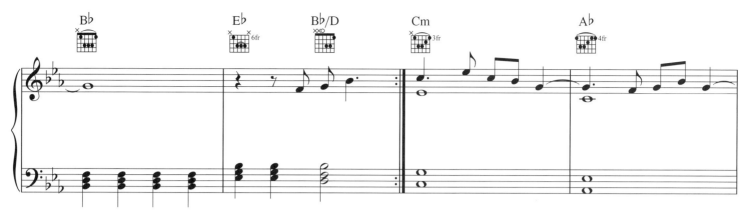

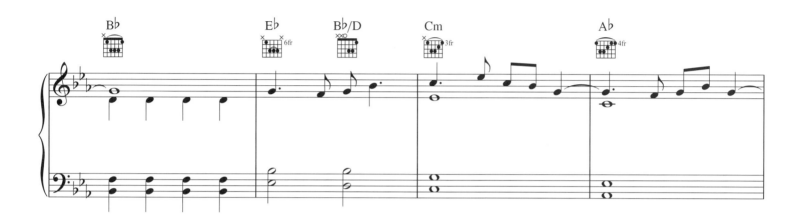

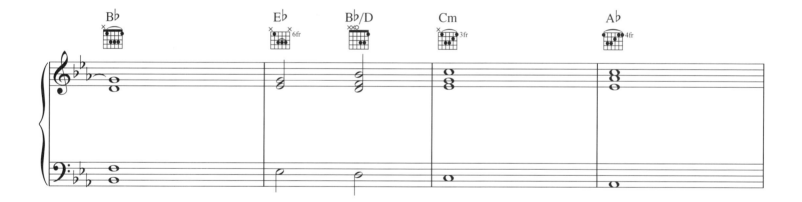

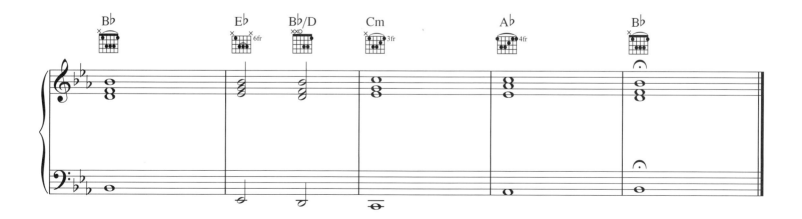

WE ARE WARRIORS
(Warrior)

Words and Music by AVRIL LAVIGNE,
CHAD KROEGER and TRAVIS CLARK

Moderately slow

We'll pick our bat-tles 'cause we know we're gon-na win the war. ___
Like ___ vik-ings, we'll be fight-ing through the day and night. ___

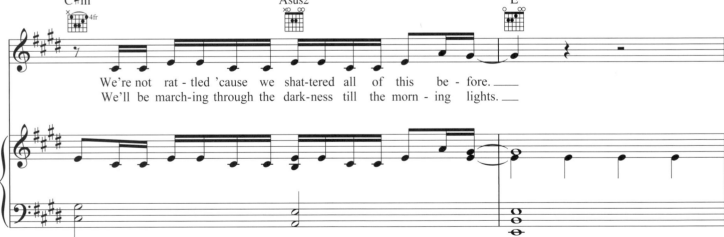

We're not rat-tled 'cause we shat-tered all of this be-fore. ___
We'll be march-ing through the dark-ness till the morn-ing lights. ___

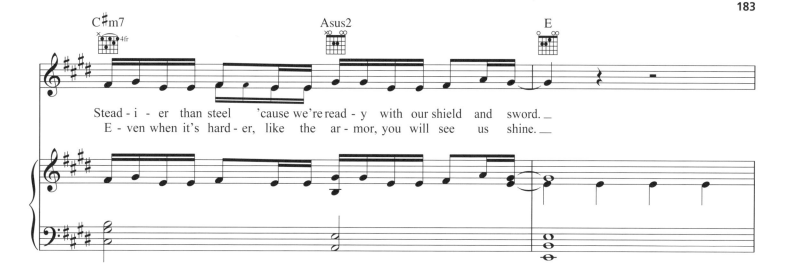

Stead - i - er than steel 'cause we're read - y with our shield and sword. __
E - ven when it's hard - er, like the ar - mor, you will see us shine. __

Back on the sad - dle 'cause we've gath-ered all our strength for more. __ And
No, we won't stop and we won't drop un - til the vic - to - ry's ours. __ No,

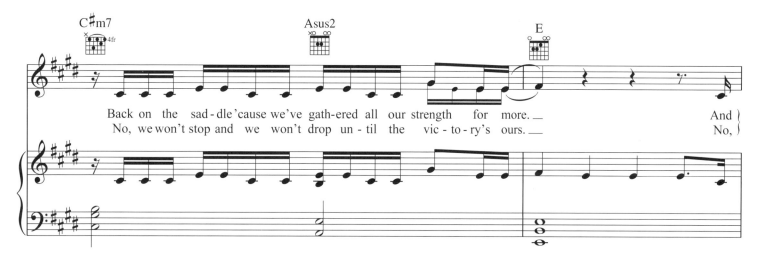

we won't bow, we won't break. No, we're not a - fraid to do what - ev - er it takes. We'll

nev - er bow, we'll nev - er break. _____ 'Cause we are

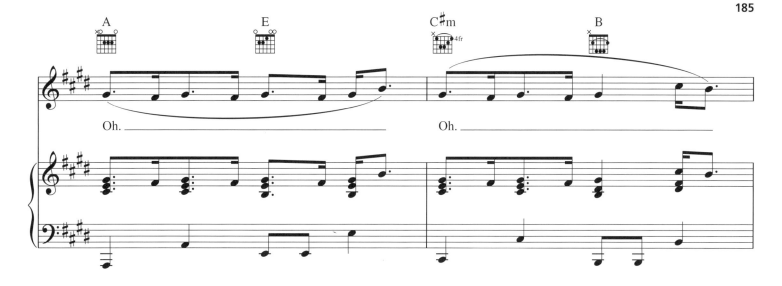

187

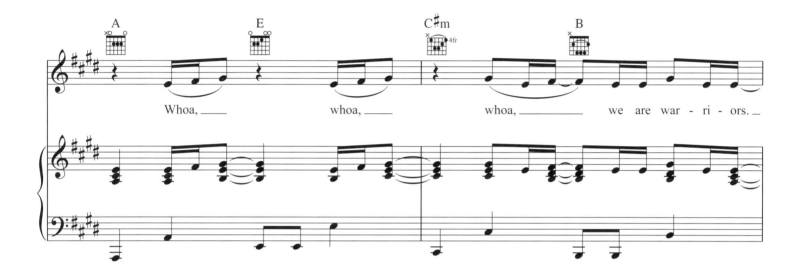

WE'RE ALL IN THIS TOGETHER

from HIGH SCHOOL MUSICAL

Words and Music by MATTHEW GERRARD
and ROBBIE NEVIL

Recorded a half step lower.

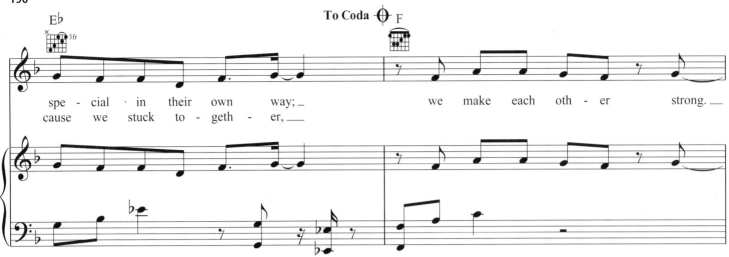

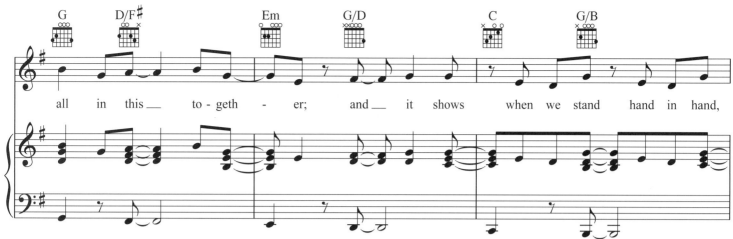

all in this __ to - geth - er; and __ it shows when we stand hand in hand,

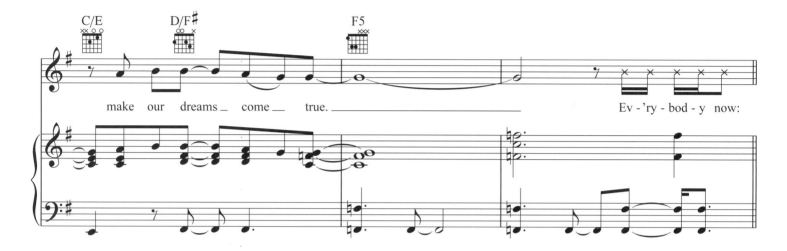

make our dreams __ come __ true. _____ Ev - 'ry - bod - y now:

To - geth - er, to - geth - er, to - geth - er, ev - 'ry - one.
To - geth - er, we're there __ for each oth - er ev - 'ry time.

To - geth - er, to - geth - er, c' - mon, __ let's have some fun.
To - geth - er, to - geth - er,

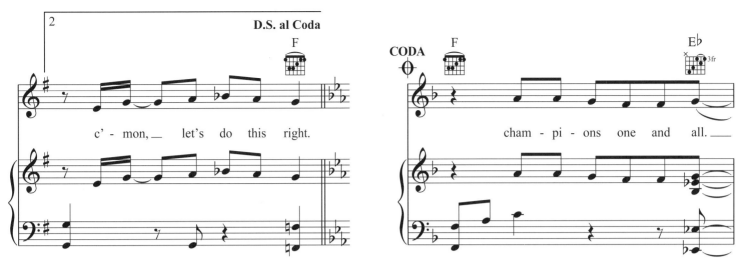

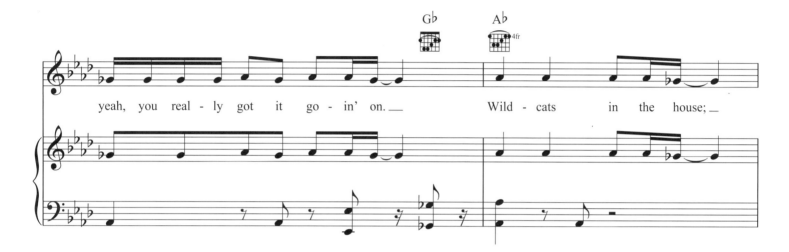

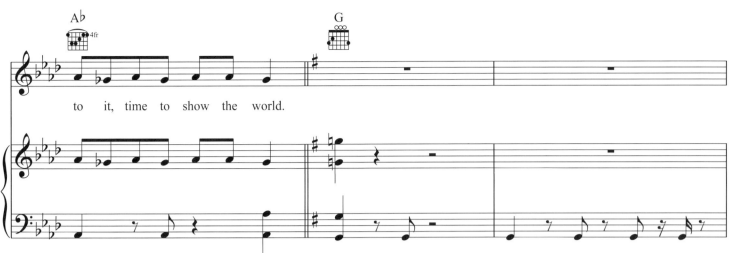

to it, time to show the world.

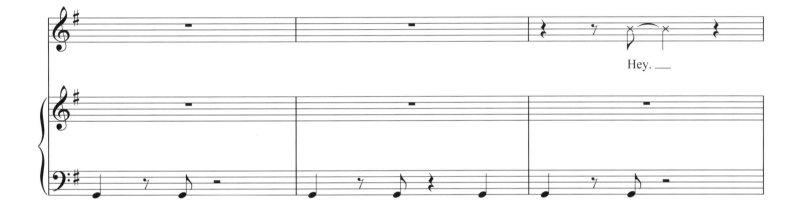

Hey. ___

Oh. ___ Hey, ___ oh, ___ al - right, here we go. We're

all in this ___ to - geth - er; once __ we know __ that we are, we're all stars,
all in this ___ to - geth - er; when __ we reach, __ we can fly, know in - side

and we see ___ that. We're all in this ___ to - geth - er; and ___ it shows
we can make ___ it. We're all in this ___ to - geth - er; once ___ we see

when we stand hand in hand, make our dreams ___ come... We're
there's a chance that we have, and we take ___ it.

Wild - cats ev - 'ry - where, ___ wave your hands up in the air. ___

That's the way we do it; let's get to it, c' - mon ___ ev - 'ry - one! ___

WITH A LITTLE HELP FROM MY FRIENDS

Words and Music by JOHN LENNON
and PAUL McCARTNEY

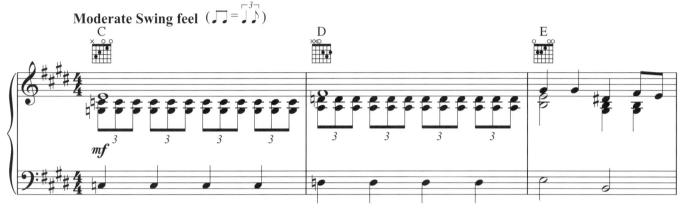

What would you think _ if I sang _ out of tune, _ would you stand _
What do I do _ when my love _ is a - way? (Does it wor -
(Would you be - lieve _ in a love _ at first sight?) _ Yes, I'm cer -

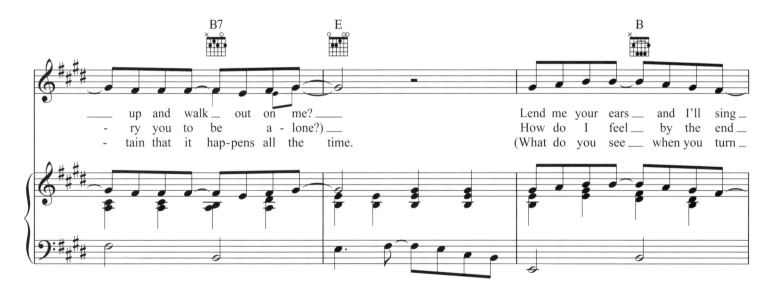

_ up and walk _ out on me? _
- ry you to be a - lone?) _
- tain that it hap-pens all the time.

Lend me your ears _ and I'll sing _
How do I feel _ by the end _
(What do you see _ when you turn _

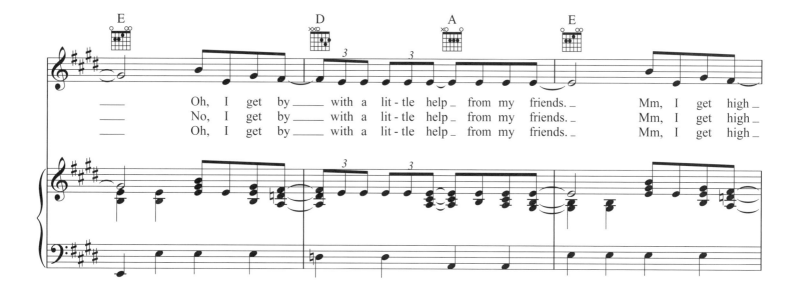

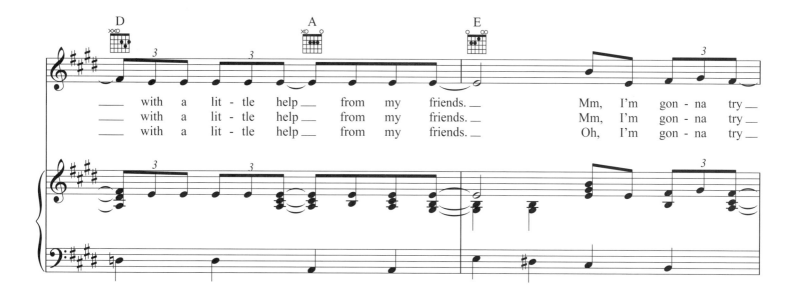

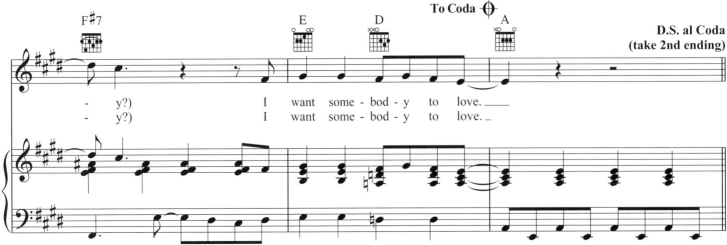

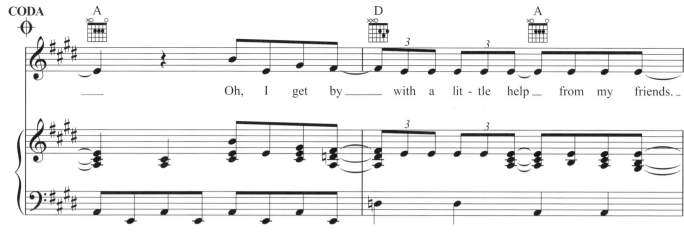

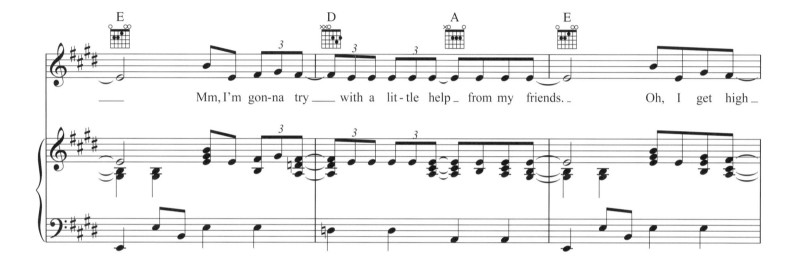

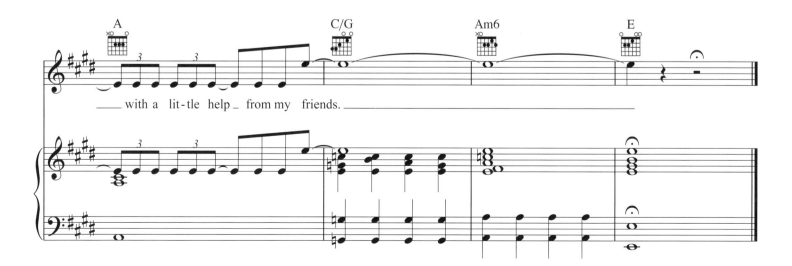

YOU WILL BE FOUND

from DEAR EVAN HANSEN

Music and Lyrics by BENJ PASEK
and JUSTIN PAUL

Recorded a half step lower.

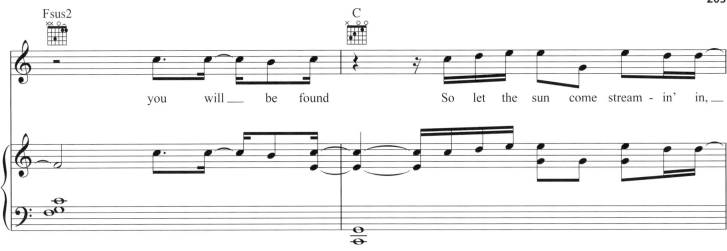

you will be found So let the sun come stream - in' in, —

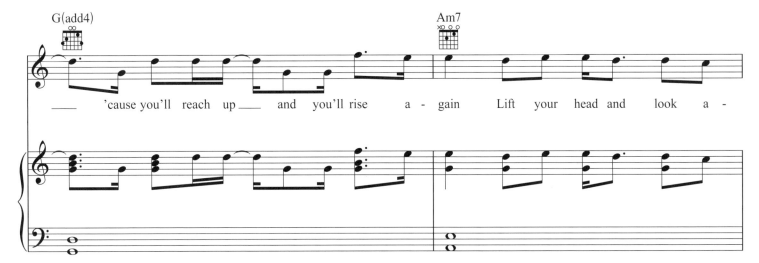

— 'cause you'll reach up — and you'll rise a - gain Lift your head and look a -

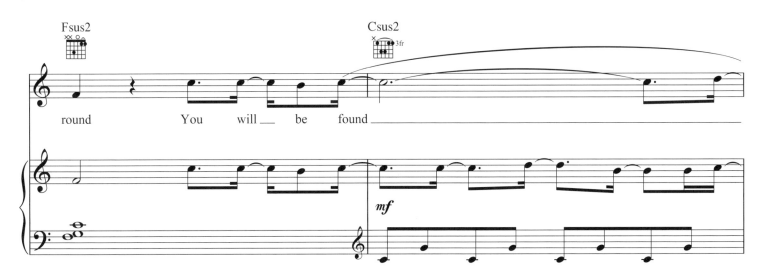

round You will — be found —

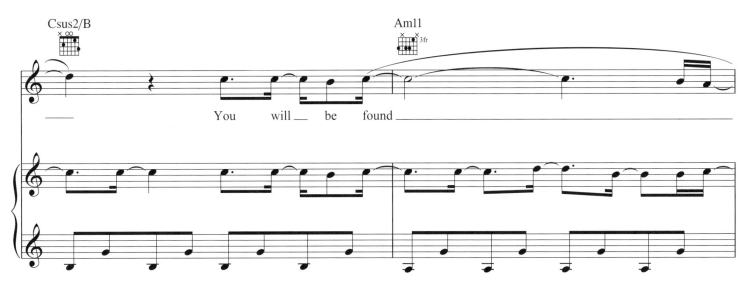

— You will — be found —

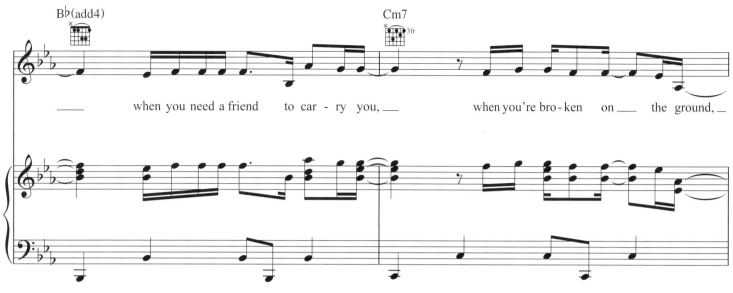

when you need a friend to car-ry you, ___ when you're bro-ken on ___ the ground, ___

___ you will ___ be found ___ So let the sun come stream-in' in, ___

___ 'cause you'll reach up ___ and you'll rise a-gain ___ If you on-ly look ___ a-round, ___

morn-ing is break-ing, and all _____ is new, _____ all _____

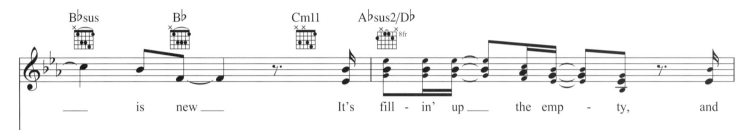

_____ is new _____ It's fill-in' up _____ the emp-ty, and

sud-den-ly _____ I see _____ that all _____ is new, _____ all _____

_____ is new.

ALANA & JARED:

You are not _____ a-lone _____

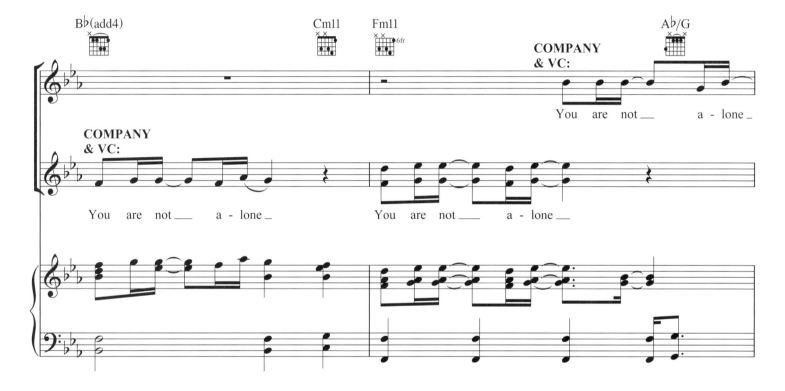

'cause you'll reach up ___ and you'll rise a - gain ___ If you on - ly look ___ a - round,

COMPANY & VC:
You will ___ be found. ___

ZOE & EVAN:
___ E - ven when the dark comes crash - ing through, ___

___ You will ___ be found ___

When you need some - one to car - ry you, ___

YOU'VE GOT A FRIEND

Words and Music by
CAROLE KING

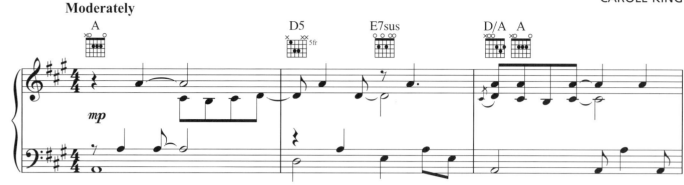

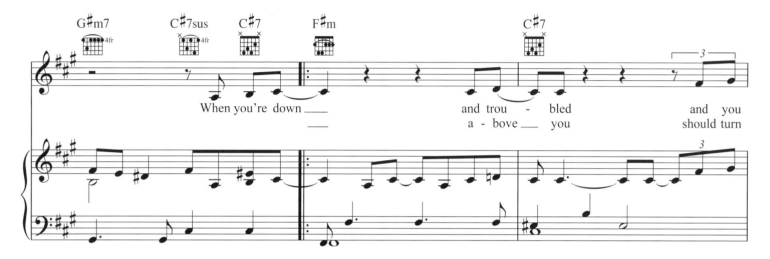

When you're down ___ and trou - bled and you
a - bove ___ you should turn

need a help-ing hand ___ and noth-ing, whoa,
dark and full of clouds ___ and that old north

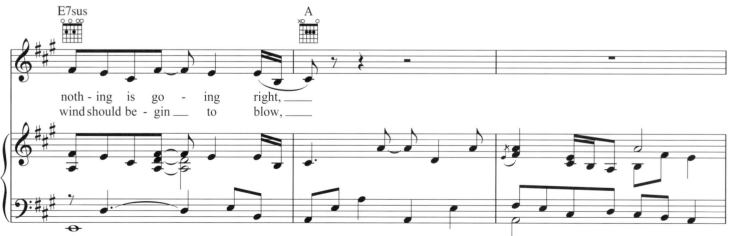

noth - ing is go - ing right, ___
wind should be - gin to blow, ___

* Cues 2nd time only

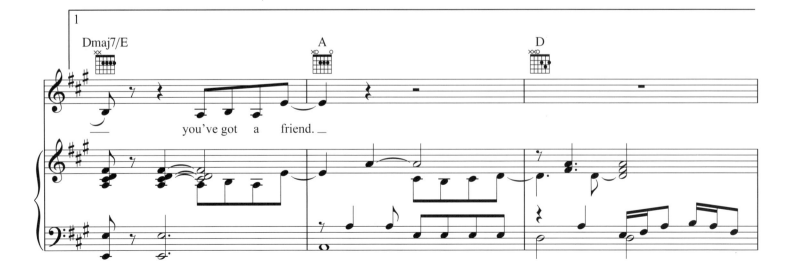

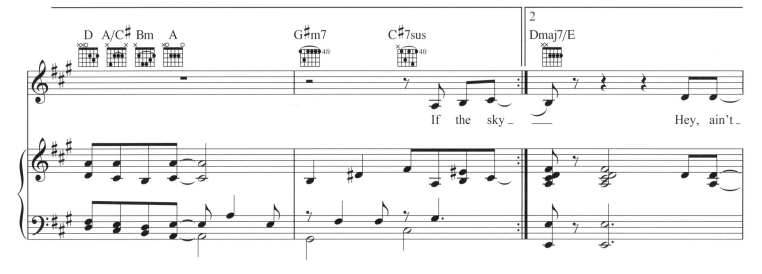

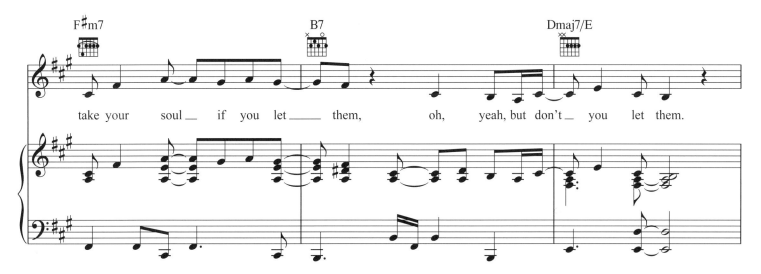

Lord, I'll be _____ there, _ yes, I will, _ Lord, _ you've got a friend. _

_____ You've _ got a friend, _ yeah.

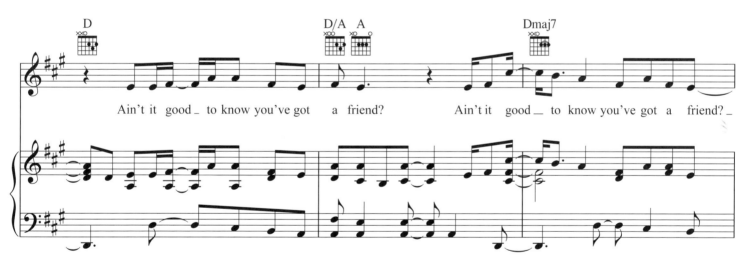

Ain't it good _ to know you've got _ a friend? Ain't it good _ to know you've got a friend? _

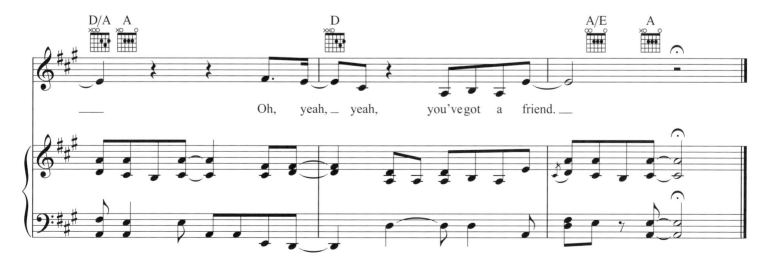

_____ Oh, yeah, _ yeah, you've got a friend. _____

YOU'LL NEVER WALK ALONE
from CAROUSEL

Lyrics by OSCAR HAMMERSTEIN II
Music by RICHARD RODGERS

Andantino molto cantabile

(with great warmth, like a hymn)

*alternate lyric: hold your head up high

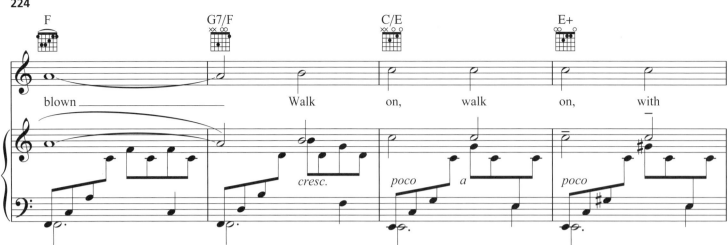

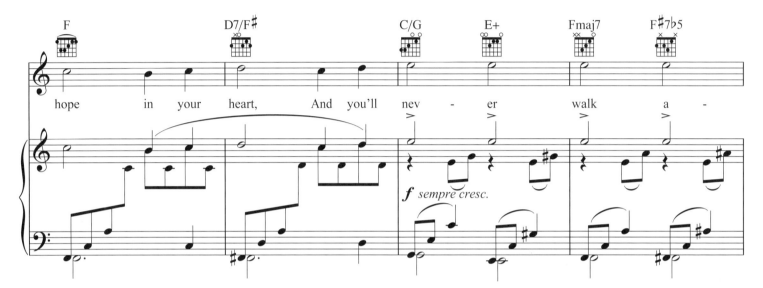

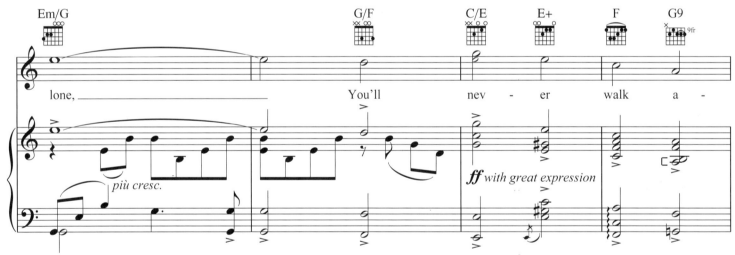

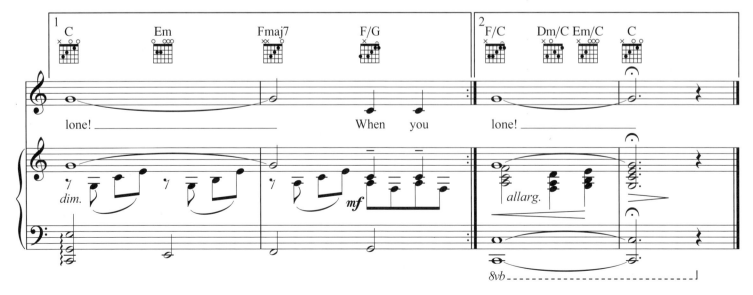